OLYMPIA
COMPLETE GUIDE

OLYMPIA
COMPLETE GUIDE

TEXT
SPYROS PHOTINOS

ENGLISH TRANSLATION
TINA McGEORGE AND COLIN MACDONALD

"OLYMPIC PUBLICATIONS"
PAN. & THEO. AGRIDIOTIS, SKOUFA 56 - ATHENS
ATHENS 1982

INTRODUCTION

I N THE western Peloponnese, in a peaceful, idyllic valley, between Kronos Hill and the confluence of the rivers Alpheios
and Kladeos, there flourished in ancient times one of the most
important panhellenic sanctuaries : the Sanctuary of Olympia. At
this Sanctuary, apart from rituals performed for healing, games
called *Olympic* were also established from a very early period and,
with the passage of time, attracted the attention of all the Greeks.
With the Olympic Games, the ideal of noble rivalry found its
complete expression and for many centuries forged the unity and
peace of the Greek world. Hence the Sanctuary where they took
place was recognised as one of the greatest panhellenic centres.

THE LEGEND

It has not yet been established when people first began worship-
ping at Olympia. However, archaeological finds show that the area
was at least settled from the 3rd millenium B.C. It is also known
that the first Sanctuary was the Gaion, which was found at the
foot of Kronos Hill and was dedicated to Geia (Earth), the wife
of Ouranos (Heaven). That was also, it is said, the most ancient
oracle of Olympia (Pausanias V,14,10).

Later, Kronos — the youngest son of Geia and Ouranos —
having deposed his father, was worshipped at Olympia with his
wife, Rhea. According to Pausanias (V,7,6) *the people of that
time, who were also called the people of the golden age, built a
shrine to Kronos at Olympia.* Besides, on the summit of Kronos
Hill which took this name from Kronos, there was an altar to the
god, where the so-called «Basilai» every year made sacrifices in
his honour (Pausanias VI, 20, 1).

In the course of the centuries came new gods. According to myth, Kronos swallowed his male children fearing that they might

5

depose him, as he had deposed Ouranos. He had devoured two children, Poseidon and Hades, when Zeus was born. Then Rhea, having given Kronos a stone bound in swaddling clothes to swallow, handed the newborn child to five Cretan brothers, the Daktyloi of Ida or Kouretes, to conceal him and bring him up in Crete.

When Zeus came of age, he asked Metis for help to overthrow Kronos. Metis gave Kronos some medicine to drink and so made him vomit the two children whom he had devoured. Then Zeus, helped by his two brothers and three sisters : Hera, Hestia and Demeter, deposed Kronos after a terrible conflict lasting ten years, which is known as the Titanomachia (Battle between the Gods and the Titans).

Since the Olympian gods prevailed, from then on the Sanctuary of Olympia became positively the Sanctuary of Zeus. So in a series of local myths Zeus was associated with Olympia and the Games. One of these local myths says that the five Cretan brothers, the Kouretes, to whom Rhea had entrusted his guardianship, came from Crete to Olympia, where Zeus was weaned on the milk of Amalthea by the nymphs. At Olympia, the eldest of the five brothers, Hercules — not Hercules the son of Amphitrion and Alkmene — arranged foot races among his brothers and honoured the winner with a crown of wild olive which grew abundantly in the valley. Even Hercules called these games «Olympic» and appointed that they should take place every fifth year, since he and his brothers numbered five (Pausanias V,7,6-9).

Other local myths also say that Zeus fought with Kronos at Olympia usurping the leadership and that he himself established the games because he overcame Kronos. It is also said that other gods competed at Olympia and that Apollo beat Ares at Boxing and outran Hermes (Pausanias V,7,10).

According to tradition Aethlios, the first king of Elis was also an organiser of the games. Aethlios was succeeded by his son Endymion, who in turn organised races at Olympia among his sons Paeon, Aetolus and Epeios, in order to leave his kingdom to the winner. Pelops too, after he beat King Oinomaos of Pisa in a chariot race and married the King's daughter Hippodameia, once again arranged at Olympia games in honour of Zeus, which it was said were the most memorable of all those which had been celebrated up till then. When Augeias reigned over Elis, Hercules — son of Amphitrion and Alkmene — came to clean his stables. After the contest however, Augeias refused to give Hercules the cattle which he had promised. Then Hercules marched against Augeias, and after conquering Elis, he arranged games at Olympia in honour of Zeus. At these games it is said that he himself was distinguished in Wrestling and in the Pankration. Finally, games at Olympia were also arranged by Oxylos, the King of Elis. After the reign of Oxylos however, the games were forgotten until the time of Iphitos, the great King of Elis (Pausanias V,8,1-5).

THE SACRED TRUCE

According to an old theory, at the beginning of the 9th century B.C., probably in 884 B.C., or according to a recent theory, in the 8th century B.C., most probably in 776 B.C., Iphitos, the King of Elis, asked the Delphic oracle to tell him what he should do to save Greece which was then scourged with civil wars and plague. Phoebus gave the reply : *Iphitos and the Eleians must revive the Olympic Games* (Pausanias V,4,6). Thus the revival of the Olympic Games was forecast as a divine request which was fulfilled by Iphitos.

At the same period, three Kings, Iphitos, Lycourgos the mythical lawgiver of Sparta and Kleosthenes of Pisa achieved the greatest peace triumph of antiquity. They concluded a lasting treaty, the Sacred Truce, which remained ever respected by all Greeks, and was as valid as a rule of international law even during the most dramatic conflicts of the ancient world. The Sacred Truce was immortalised by the Eleians on a bronze disc, the so-called Disc of Iphitos, which was kept in the Temple of Hera, where Pausanias saw it in 160 A.D. and described it (Pausanias V,20,1).

By the Sacred Truce, the district of Olympia and Elis was declared sacrosanct and inviolable, the entrance of an army or even of armed men on to its ground was forbidden and it was initially legislated that wars and hostilities should cease for a month — the Sacred Month when the Olympic Games were celebrated — and later for three months. Thus the athletes, the representatives of the various cities and the multitudinous pilgrims were able to go to Olympia and return to their homes unhindered and in safety.

The Sacred Truce which was proclaimed in all Greek cities by representatives from Elis, the Spondophoroi (bearers of the peace treaty), endowed the Sanctuary at Olympia with a high prestige, which was both impressive and important ; in this way it succeeded for many centuries in preserving both youthful and flourishing the Olympic Games.

The peace-bearing proclamation of Olympia had the power to soften animosity, to neutralise evil, to unite enemy camps, to create brotherhood on the field of battle, to stop wars and hostilities and to pacify the whole of the Greek world. The Greek world, with its profound religious faith, rendered to this divine proclamation the respect which it deserved and rarely allowed the Truce to be violated.

Moreover, those, either cities or individuals, who violated the Truce, were punished by the Olympic Council with severe penalties and heavy fines. To those who did not pay the fine, or until the fine was paid, the Delphic oracle did not give divinations, while the Olympic Council excluded them from the panhellenic celebration of the Olympic Games. Concerning this, it is recorded that in 420 B.C. Sparta refused to pay the fine which had been

7

imposed on her because her army had occupied the small city of Lepreon during the Truce. She was then excluded from the Olympic Games and she was only allowed to take part after evacuating Lepreon and depositing the part of the fine which was due to the Sanctuary. It is even reported that during the reign of Philip II of Macedon, while the Sacred Truce was in force, Phrynon, an Athenian citizen, was robbed by Macedonian hoplites. Then Philip, though maintaining that his hoplites did not know that the Truce had been announced, asked for the pardon of the Olympic Council.

THE BEGINNING OF GREEK HISTORY

With the reorganisation of the Games which was accomplished by Iphitos, the Sanctuary of Olympia began to develop and gradually to acquire panhellenic authority. From then on the Olympic Games continued to take place every four years without interruption.

It seems that at the same time the names of the winners began to be recorded, as well as the corresponding Olympiads, for it is known that each Olympiad took the name of the winner of the Stade race, that is the winner of the ordinary foot race. This preference for the winner of the Stade race, who each time gave his name to the Olympiad, is due to the fact that the Stade was the most ancient competition and the only one until 728 B.C.

Over the passage of the centuries, a whole series of Stade race winners were recorded, whose names represented a corresponding series of Olympiads. Thus at the end of the 5th century B.C., for the first time the sophist, Hippias the Eleian, probably using the Sanctuary archives, the inscriptions on the statues of the winners and local traditions, drew up a list of Olympic winners and numbered the Olympiads up to his day. This list was supplemented by Aristotle and other writers with the later Olympiads. According to this register, the first Olympiad is that in which the Stade race was won by Koroibos of Elis — that is why it is called the Koroibos Olympiad — and its conventional date is the year 776 B.C.

It is worth noting that the Olympiads, the four yearly intervals which separated two successive celebrations of the Olympic Games, were used to date historical events. For example the Battle of Thermopylae is recorded as having taken place during the first year of the 75th Olympiad, that is 480 B.C.

Chronology was simplified by the numbering of the Olympiads in the register of Hippias, and also by the division of each into 4 years and of each year into months, a fact which was known to all Greeks. Thus, with the system of the Olympiads, the old means of dating, which used various local registers (such as the names of the Athenian rulers, or Spartan Ephors and so on), were gradually replaced. Thus the events of a period of 1168 years, the period from the first to the last (293rd), Olympiad (776 B.C. - 393 A.D.), were dated.

This system was used for the first time at the end of the 4th century B.C. by Timaeus and later by Polybius, Diodorus the Sicilian and other authors. These authors dated the historical events of their time according to Olympiads, but at the same time they put in order the various Olympiads and the historical events of the previous centuries, which were dated according to local registers. The transfer of chronology from local registers to the corresponding Olympiads was done methodically and went back to the Ist Olympiad (in 776 B.C.), which now consitutes the point at which historical times in Greece begin. So one can understand how the historical beginning of the Olympic Games, in the year 776 B.C., coincides with the beginning of Greek history.

When exactly the Olympic Games took place is not known according to the modern calendar. It is known, however, that they took place during a season of great heat and always when there was a full-moon. It is also known that the Olympiad was «five-yearly», which means that the games took place at the beginning of every fifth year, that is after the passage of a full four years since the previous games.

According to one theory, the Olympic Games took place every 49 and 50 months alternately. Thus *«when its celebration fell in the month of Apollonios it would next be celebrated after four years in the month of Parthenios, which came after the month of Apollonios»* (G. Thomson — Aeschylus and Athens). There are many opinions about which months correspond to the ancient months of Apollonios and Parthenios. However, it seems most probable that they correspond to July and August.

THE HERAIA

Apart from the games for men, which were arranged in honour of Zeus, the Heraia, foot races in honour of Hera had been established from very early times. According to Pausanias Hippodameia was the first to organise the Heraia *in gratitude to Hera for her marriage to Pelops* (Pausanias V,16,4).

Only virgins from Elis were permitted to take part in these races. They did not run the whole length of the Stadium, but only about 160 metres, wearing their hair loose and a short tunic with the hem above the knee and the right shoulder bare to the breast. The winners had the right to dedicate their statues to the Heraion (Temple of Hera), and received for a prize a crown of wild olive and a portion of the meat of the cow sacrifices to Hera.

The judges of the Heraia were 16 Eleian women, who every four years wove the sacred peplos (form of dress), of Hera, and during the ceremony of the Heraia, laid it at the cult statue of the goddess in the Heraion. These women honoured Hera with two

9

dances, that of Hippodameia and that of Physkoa. The first is named after the well-known heroine of the East Pediment of the
Temple of Zeus, who as mentioned, established the Heraia, and
the second is a local nymph with whom the god Dionysus fell in
love.

The games and festivals of the Heraia did not take place at the
same time as the Olympic Games, but an interval of time always
separated them. According to one theory the alternation of the
Olympic Games to take place in every Apollonios and Parthenios
month was on account of the Heraia. So, if the Heraia consistently
took place in the month of Parthenios, the Olympic Games took
place on one occasion before them and on the next occasion after
them, so that this women's festival would not lose its significance.

THE PANHELLENIC OLYMPIC GAMES

The Panhellenic Olympic Games grew out of a festival of local
character. However, it seems that the Truce, which was established by the largest cities of the Peloponnese, was initiated by the
panpeloponnesian games which in the course of time became panhellenic and attracted the attention of the whole of the then known
world, whither the Greeks had spread.

The Ionian cities of Asia Minor, Cyprus together with other
Greek Islands, the colonies of the Pontus, North Africa, Magna
Graecia, as well as the cities of continental Greece joyfully received the Olympic proclamation of peace. Thus the Sanctuary of
Olympia rapidly became the most enviable panhellenic religious
and competitive centre. Moreover, the Olympic Games really idea-
lised Greek Life. They represented a lofty ideal which for many
centuries inspired the youth of ancient times, an ideal which, through honourable and noble competition, sought to develop the
mind and strengthen the body in order to create a superior character.

*

The radiant spirit of Olympia gradually diffused to all Greek cities. The fact that the Olympics were celebrated in honour of
Zeus, the great god of all the Greeks, consolidated their religious
importance. Moreover, the principle of the Sanctuary was not to
debase the religious concept of the contests at Olympia by awar-
ding a monetary prize to the winner, but by preserving «crowning», to ensure the moral superiority of the Olympics as contests
of virtue.

The Olympic Games did not award money or silver but crowns.
The winners received only a crown of wild olive, plaited from a
branch of the sacred tree, the «Olive of Kallistephanos» (beautiful
crown). The Olive of Kallistephanos grew near the opisthodomos

of the Temple of Zeus, next to the altar of the Nymphs of Kalli-stephanos. After a sacrifice was made on this altar, a child both of whose parents were living, climbed up the sacred tree and with a golden knife cut branches to be made into the crowns of the victors. Some say that the Kallistephanos Olive was brought as a plant by Hercules from the land of the Hyperboreas (Far North), and others say that after a prediction made by the Delphic oracle to Iphitos, King of Elis, the sacred tree was found wrapped in a cobweb, in the opisthodomos of the Temple of Zeus.

In the earlier Olympic Games the prize was an apple or a bronze tripod. However, from the 7th Olympiad (752 B.C.), they started to crown the winners. During this Olympiad the Messenian Daikles, who won the Stade race, was the first Olympic victor to be honoured with the crown of the wild olive.

The crown of the wild olive was the most idolised aspiration of Greek youth. This clearly shows that for the Greeks the contest did not take place either for simple exhibition, or riches, but for spiritual improvement, for the harmonious development of body and mind, for the worship of beauty and nobility. In the Stadium of Olympia displays of strength had to be combined completely with good character and a cultivated mind. That was the ideal aim of the Olympic Games : the harmonious existence, within the same individual, of virtue and strength, for the creation of spiritual and bodily perfection and of a generation endowed with virtue and strength.

Herodotus, the Father of History, expresses the profound meaning of the Olympic Games very well, when describing the conversation of Xerxes, Mardonius and other Persian officers with some Greek deserters who went from the Arcadians to the Persian camp after the Battle of Thermopylae. Once they had explained, it says, that the Greeks at that time held *contests for athletes and horse races* at Olympia, Xerxes, being curious, asked what were the prizes for the winners. They replied : *a crown of wild olive.* Then a staff officer, Tritandaechmes, son of Artabanus, spoke to Mardonius who had induced the Persian king to campaign against Greece and said : *Alas, Mardonius, against whom have you brought us to fight ? With men who compete not for money but for virtue.* (Herodotus Book VIII, 26).

*

The ideals to which the Olympic Games aspired are verified by the strict rules for the athletes taking part. The athletes had to be Greek freemen — slaves were forbidden to take part — who had not commited any crime or impious act, broken the rules of the Games or the Truce. In addition, they had to have trained in their place of origin for ten months before the Games, and during the last month, in Elis or Olympia.

11

Elis was a very ancient city built on the left bank of the Peneios river. It was unwalled and had some notable public buildings. It had four gymnasiums for training athletes, a building for the Hellanodikai (Umpires) where they were taught their responsibilities by the Thesmophylakes or Gaurdians of the Law ; there was also a important theatre and Bouleuterion and a special house for the sixteen Eleian women who every four years wove the sacred peplos of Hera and organised the Heraia.

This city-state, which lay about fifty kilometres from Olympia — near modern Amaliada — had overall control of the Sanctuary and, from its great priestly families, the Iamides and Klytiades, it appointed its priests alternately. Also, the Council (Boule) of Eleians organised the Olympic Games, and while they were in progress, met in the Bouleuterion at Olympia. This is why it is called the Olympic Council.

The control which the Eleians exercised over the Sanctuary was the cause of a long and enduring quarrel between them and Pisa, a neighbouring city of Olympia to which the Sanctuary originally belonged. The discord which broke out from time to time developed into bloody conflicts between the two cities in 572 and 472 B.C., the result being the defeat of the Pisans and the destruction of their city. The last vain attempt of the Pisans was in 364 B.C. However, the Olympiads which had been supervised by the Pisans in 748, 644 and 364 B.C. were not recognised by the Eleians who called then non-Olympiads.

However, after the destruction of Pisa, Elis permanently supervised the Sanctuary and the Games. The wise administration of the city always had at its disposal the impartial judges, the Hellanodikai who were entrusted with the smooth running of the Games and the rigid application of the rules. In this task they were assisted by a corps of officials (a kind of police force) the Alytai, the lictors, the flagellators and so on, who were directed by the Alytarch (chief of the Alytai).

The Hellanodikai were Eleian citizens elected by lot for a single Olympiad, and while performing their duties they wore an imposing purple cloak. Among their various responsibilities, was the enforcing of severe penalties for people who violated regulations, and also the prize-giving for the winners. Their decisions were always respected, even in cases where they were clearly unjustified. Those who maintained that they had been wronged could appeal to the Olympic Council which had the power to punish the Hellanodikai severely. But these rules were rarely applied because the Hellanodikai always judged fairly and with impartiality, virtues which were recognised by all the Greeks and which maintained the high prestige of the Olympic Games.

The numbers of Hellanodikai changed at different times corresponding to the number of clans of Eleians. However, in 348 B.C.

it was established that there should be ten, and this number remained constant until the very last Olympiad.

*

The events which were included in the Olympic programme can be divided into althletic and equestrian contests. The former were held in the Stadium and the latter in the Hippodrome. The competitors in the athletic events were divided according to age into men and boys, and those in the equestrian contests, into chariot races and horse races.

The most ancient athletic event was the Stade race which was run the length of the Stadium, that is 192.25 m., and was the only contest until 728 B.C. From then on, the number of competitions gradually increased.

724 B.C.: Diaulos or two-stade race (192.25 m. x 2).

720 B.C.: Dolichos, that is the distance of 24 stades (192.25 m. x 24).

708 B.C.: Wrestling and Pentathlon. The Pentathlon comprised the following events : long jump, discus, javelin, running and wrestling.

688 B.C.: Boxing.

648 B.C.: Pankration. This was a very tough and dangerous sport being a combination of wrestling and boxing.

632 B.C.: Stade race and Boys' Wrestling.

616 B.C.: Boys' Boxing.

520 B.C.: Hoplite race. This was an impressive race in which athletes ran in complete bronze armour.

200 B.C.: Finally, the Boys' Pankration.

The equestrian competitions were established in 680 B.C. with the Tethrippon (a chariot race for four horses), according to Pausanias. But according to Pindar, they were established much earlier in 740 B.C., when Samos from Mantinea won the Tethrippon. More races were introduced after that.

648 B.C.: Horse race for stallions.

408 B.C.: The Synoris or two-horse chariot race.

384 B.C.: Four-horse chariot race for one-year-olds.

268 B.C.: Two-horse chariot race for one-year-olds.

256 B.C.: Horse race for one-year-old stallions.

It is worth noting that in these games, the owners and not the charioteers were declared winners. Thus, although the presence of women at the Olympic Games was strictly forbidden, it was also possible for women to be declared winners. The first woman to be declared winner of the Tethrippon in 396 (?) and 392 B.C. was Kyniska, sister of Agesilaus II, King of Sparta, who also set up her statue in the Altis. Later on, in 268 B.C., the winner was Velestiche from Macedon, but most of the others were Spartan women.

Apart from athletics and horse events, after 396 B.C. contests for heralds and trumpeters were included in the programme. This happened in the Sacred Altis, near the entrance to the Stadium, in the space which is in front of the north side of the Echo Colonnade. According to Pausanias (V,22,1) there was an altar there which was not used for sacrifices for any god but as a Bema (rostrum) on which the heralds and trumpeters would compete. The winners of these competitions would either announce the names of other winners or sound the trumpet for different commands throughout the Games.

*

On the eve of the Olympic Games, the Hellanodikai, the athletes and their trainers would set off from Elis walking along the Sacred Way and arrive at Olympia. A little after Elis on the Sacred Way was a holy spring, Pierra, where sacrifices were made. Meantime the Theoroi, that is the delegates of the Greek cities, who followed the Games from seats of honour and finally the crowds of pilgrims would arrive. After a little while, the great festival of Greece would begin.

Originally, the games would only last one day. However, when new events were established later on and word of these had spread, other days were added. Thus from 680 B.C. they lasted two days, from 632 B.C., three, and from 472 B.C. five days.

On the first day of the festival, the athletes were registered in the Bouleuterion. There, in front of the statue of Zeus Orkios, the Guardian of Oaths who held thunderbolts in his hands, oaths would be taken when a boar had been sacrificed. The athletes would swear that they had trained for ten months and that they would compete fairly, abiding by the rules. As well as the athletes, their fathers, brothers and trainers also had to swear and maintain that the athletes had, in fact, trained together according to the rules and that they had all the qualifications which allowed them a place in the Games. Finally, the Hellanodikai would take their oaths to judge the Games with impartiality. After the oaths, the contests of the heralds and trumpeters would take place, followed by those of the boys.

The start of the Games in the Stadium had a particularly festive character, since the Hellanodikai and athletes always entered by the official entrance, the Krypte, marching slowly and with dignity according to Philostratos. There they were met by the priestess of the goddess Demeter Chamyne, the only woman who could lawfully attend the Games, and by the masses of spectators. And when everything was ready, the herald would proclaim the great Olympic message to all the Greeks that the Games were beginning.

On the second day, the horse races took place in the Hippodrome, and afterwards, the Pentathlon in the Stadium.

The third day was the most splendid of the Games. In the morning of that day, the priests, the Hellanodikai, the athletes and trainers, the lords of Elis and even the delegates from the Greek cities formed a procession which set out from the Prytaneion going along the Processional way, entered the Sacred Altis from the South Processional Gate, passed in front of the east side of the Temple of Zeus and arrived at the Great Altar of Zeus. There a hecatomb was sacrificed to the God, that is an offering of one hundred oxen, the largest sacrifice to take place in the Sanctuary during the Games. When these acts of worship were finished, the track events were held (Stade, Diaulos and Dolichos races).

On the fourth day, the tough games took place, namely Wrestling, Boxing, the Pankration and the Hoplite race.

The prizes were awarded on the last day in the entrance of the Temple of Zeus. There, on the table of ivory and gold made by Pheidias' apprentice, Kolotis, were the garlands of wild olive. Previously, a bronze tripod had been used for same purpose. The Hellanodikai crowned the winners with these garlands while the crowd cheered and showered them with flowers and leaves.

After the prize-giving, the Eleians laid on a feast in the Prytaneion in honour of the Olympic champions, to which were invited the officials, the delegates of the Greek cities and all the distinguished people visiting the Sanctuary. Meanwhile, in the vale of Olympia, the friends, relatives and fellow citizens of the winners celebrated the victories until the following day when the return home began.

*

The Olympic Games were protected with laws so strictly enforced that the high standards of the competitions were maintained. Athletes who transgressed these rules were punished with fines, disqualification or public flogging, according to the gravity of the offence.

An infringement which the Hellanodikai punished with suitable harshness was bribery since it was in total contrast to the original spirit of the Olympic Games, namely to compete with honour. That is why all those who bribed their opponents so that they could win, and also those who accepted money to lose, were banned from competing and had to pay heavy fines. With these fines, they contributed to the cost of the Zanes, the statues of Zeus which stood by the official entrance to the Stadium as a warning to the athletes. On the statues themselves were written various didactic epigrams. One of these told how *the Olympic victor must win not with money but with fleetness of foot and strength of body,* and another how *these statues teach all Greeks not to offer money to win an Olympic event.* (Pausanias V,21,4).

In 388 B.C., the first penalty for bribery was imposed, and with the fines which the offenders paid the first six Zanes were made and erected in front of the entrance to the Stadium. This severe penalty acted as a deterent maintaining the ancient tradition of the Games until 332 B.C. The feeling of Greek world and the cities stopped this means of payment because the punishment of the athletes ruined the reputation of their native city. In 332 B.C., after the second case of bribery, six other Zanes were set up while in the Roman period, more were added making a total of sixteen.

Until the start of the 4th century B.C. the ideal of honourable competition prevailed at Olympia without exception. The athletes entered the arena with the noble dream of victory. However, they fully realized that a victory is not won with money and that only by long hours of practice and persistent effort could they triumph. That is why the Olympic winners became symbols of strength and virtue in every clan and every city, and were respected throughout the whole of Greece. This explains why the winners could dine free at the Prytaneion in Athens and why Solon established a monetary prize for those of his fellow citizens who by victory brought honour to the city. Again, in Sparta, it was usual for the king to fight with a crowned victor by his side. In every Greek city there was the fine tradition of pulling down part of the walls so that an Olympic winner could return home in a four-horse chariot because, according to Plutarch, *walls are of little use to a town when its citizens can fight and win.*

A separate honour for a champion was that an ode be written for him by a famous poet such as Simonides, Bacchylides or Pindar who would celebrate their virtue and courage. However, the greatest of all honours was that a statue of himself could be dedicated in the Sacred Altis. Down the centuries, inscribed on the base of the statue was his name and that of his father and city. The first statues of Olympic winners to be set up in the Sanctuary were those of Praxidamas of Aegina who won the Boxing in 544 B.C. and Opountios Rexivios who won the Pankration in 536 B.C. They were made of wood, the one of cypress and the other of fig. From then on, little by little, the Sacred Altis became crowded with hundreds of statues of Olympic victors.

*

The severity of the rules of the Olympic Games were not only restricted to athletes, trainers and the Hellanodikai, but extended to the spectators who were not allowed to be slaves or anyone guilty of impious acts. Barbarians (non-Greeks), however, could watch the Games.

Women were also forbidden to watch the Games. However, Pausanias tells us that this prohibition only extended to married women. It is a difficult problem whether or not maidens were allowed to attend the Games since the Heraia had been established for them. Moreover, in the equestrian events, women could enter teams and charioteers and could even be declared winners, for, as already mentioned, in those events, the owners and not the charioteers were awarded the prize.

All women who violated the above rules were thrown over the edge of Typaion, the mountain which lies to the south-east of Olympia beyond the Alpheios. There is no historical source which could verify that this harsh penalty was ever imposed. Nevertheless, it was said that a Rhodian woman, Pherenike or, according to others, Kallipateira, daughter of the Olympic champion Diagoras, brought her son, Peisirodos to Olympia to take part in the boys' events because her husband had died. Being very crafty, the Rhodian woman disguised herself as a male trainer and, together with the others, entered the Stadium unnoticed. Her son was declared winner and his mother, so overwhelmed with joy, ran to Peisirodos. But, as she leapt into the arena, her tunic caught on the fence revealing that she was, in fact, female. Then she was arrested and brought before the Hellanodikai to be tried according to law. However, out of respect for her father, her three brothers and her son, her life was spared, for all were Olympic champions. After this episode, which probably took place in 396 B.C., they made a law which obliged the trainers to enter the Stadium naked like the athletes.

It is said that Fate kept a beautiful death in store for Diagoras, Pherenike's father, the most renowned boxer in Greece. In 448 B.C., then an old man, he came to Olympia as a distinguished champion and had the joy of seeing his sons, Akousilaos and Damagetos, both win on the same day, the one in the Pankration and the other in Boxing. In the hour of triumph, the sons of this Olympic champion, ran to their father and crowned him with their garlands and, raising him on their shoulders, carried him round in the crowd. And while the crowd cheered and applauded with frantic enthusiasm, showering the happy father with flowers, a Spartan roared in a thunderous voice : *Die now Diagoras, you will not ascend to Olympus*. In other words you will not become a god, but this honour is enough for you. A little while later, Diagoras was dead on the shoulders of his children.

*

Apart from the representatives of the Greek cities, great politicians, famous generals, previous Olympic winners, philosophers, orators and intellectuals were always present at the Olympic Games and its various rituals. This panhellenic gathering gave them all the opportunity to communicate with the Greeks, but also gave to all the Greeks the opportunity to honour and admire their great works.

Two of the Seven Sages of ancient Greece are said to have died at an advanced age while attending the Games at Olympia : Chilon of Sparta, in 556 B.C., when overcome with great emotion as he embraced his Olympic victor son, and Thales of Miletus in 548 B.C., while watching the games in the scorching heat (Diogenes Laertios I,72 and I, 38-39).

Important philosophers like Plato and Aristotle were regular spectators at the Games ; great poets such as Simonides, Bacchylides, Pindar and others celebrated with their verses the Olympionikai (Olympic winners), and famous artists such as Pythagoras, Myron, Pheidias, Paionios, Praxiteles, Lyssipus and others adorned the Sanctuary with their masterpieces and thus became known to the ends of the world.

Great tyrants, politicians and kings themselves took part in the Games with the aim of increasing their political power through an Olympic victory. Thus the Tyrants of Syracuse Gelon and Hieron were distinguished as Olympic winners in the four-horse chariot race in 488 and 464 B.C. respectively. Later in 416 B.C., Alcibiades the Athenian politician took part in the Games with seven chariots and after being declared the winner of the four-horse chariot race, he celebrated the victory by giving a banquet for the participants in the rejoicing. Finally in 356 B.C., Philip II, King of Macedonia, father of Alexander the Great, won the horse race.

It is reported that after the Persian wars, in 476 B.C., Themistocles was also present at the most brilliant Olympics which had ever taken place. As he entered the Stadium, although the games had already begun the Greeks stopped watching them in order to cheer. That day in the Stadium the gratitude of all Greeks was concentrated on honouring the heroic victor of Salamis.

Later in 444 B.C., Herodotus read to the rejoicing crowd extracts from his histories about the victories of the Greeks over the Persians, and among others he moved the young Thucydides, afterwards himself to become a great historian.

On other occasions, chosen personalities of the ancient world, with the authority in which they were held throughout the whole of Greece, delivered the panegyrics from the Bema which had been placed for this purpose in the opisthodomos of the Temple of Zeus. In these speeches they emphasised the need for panhellenic brotherhood, especially after the catastrophic outcome of the Peloponnesian War. Thus it is clear that the Sanctuary at Olympia tried to impart to the whole of the Greek world its spirit of peace and brotherhood.

At the end of the 5th century B.C., Gorgias of Leontini was the first to raise the voice of peace on behalf of the Greeks, saying in his Olympic speech that *victories against the barbarians are worthy of anthems, but against the Greeks they are worthy of lamentations*. Later Lysias, in his Olympic oration given in 384 B.C., emphasised the peaceful and brotherly meaning of the celebrations at Olympia, saying that *he who established the games* — he meant Idaean Hercules — *believed that through them he would initiate panhellenic friendship*. Lysias, the exponent of a broader democratic ideology, even invited the Greeks to unite not only against the Persians, but also against the tyrants and in particular against Dionysios, Tyrant of Syracuse. Finally Isocrates, with the same aim, distributed at the panhellenic celebration at Olympia, in 380 B.C., copies of his panegyric in which he made an appeal to Athens and Sparta to unite and effectively confront the barbarian threat.

This idea of panhellenic unity and peace, which was persistently cultivated at all the Sanctuaries and particularly at the Sanctuary of Olympia, through the panegyrics reached the furthest corners of Greece, and though the idea was never realised, it did however help to mould the national conscience of the Greeks.

THE MACEDONIANS AND THE ROMANS

The panhellenic celebration of the Olympic Games survived and flourished from 776 B.C., which is its historical beginning, until the end of the 4th century B.C.

After the Battle of Chaeronea (338 B.C.), and the domination by the Macedonians of Greek lands, the Macedonian Kings Philip II and Alexander the Great built the Philippeion at Olympia and promoted the Sanctuary and the Games in which Philip II, in 356 B.C., had formerly been distinguished as a winner. The Greek origin of the Macedonian kings, which was an indispensible prerequisite for participation in the Olympic Games, had earlier been scrutinised when King Alexander I (498 - 454 B.C.), was accepted by the Hellanodikai having previously succeeded in proving his descent from the Temenides, an old royal line from Argos in the Peloponnese (Herodotus V, 22).

It is certain that Alexander the Great particularly respected the Sanctuary at Olympia and the Games. This explains why at Issos, during his campaign, he freed a prisoner from Thebes immediately he heard that the man was an Olympic winner. Furthermore, in 324 B.C., he chose to announce to the Greeks at Olympia his decree which gave a general amnesty to all exiles, and sent Nikanor to read it out in the crowded Stadium.

After the death of Alexander the Great the ancient splendour of the Olympic Games gradually gave way, in spite of the fact that his successors raised new monuments and supported the Sanctuary financially.

In 146 B.C. Greece was conquered by the Romans. Then, for the Olympic Games and the Sanctuary the long Roman era began which lasted several centuries. During this period the right of the Romans to participate in the Olympic Games was recognised, since it was first settled that they were of Greek origin. Thus many emperors and officers were distinguished as Olympic winners.

However, in 85 B.C., Sulla pillaged the Greek sanctuaries and in particular the Sanctuary at Olympia, because he needed money to conduct the war against Mithridates, while, in 80 B.C., in order to celebrate the triumphs of that same war the Olympic Games (175th Olympiad), were held at Rome.

During the reign of the Emperor Octavian Augustus (30 B.C. - 14 A.D.) the Sanctuary grew and revived. But later the Olympic Games experienced the vanity and imperious behaviour of the Emperor Nero. The 211th Olympiad, which should have taken place in 65 A.D., took place in 67 A.D., so that he himself could take part in them. At these Games, Nero included other contests unheard of until then in the programme of the Olympic Games and he was many times declared Olympic winner. Namely, it is reported that he won the artistic contests for tragic actors and musicians, even though *he had a voice worse than a crow's*. It is worth noting that the Eleians did not enter this Olympiad in their official register.

During the 2nd century A.D., and particularly during the reign of the philhellene Emperor Hadrian (117 - 138 A.D.), the Sanctuary revived once again. But from the 3rd century A.D., its influence was yearly more and more restricted and the Greek cities were no longer interested in the Olympic Games. However, from this period the Olympic Games acquired virtually an international character, since athletes from all of the countries of the far-flung Roman Empire (Egyptians, Phoenicians, Armenians and others), arrived at Olympia to lay claim to Olympic victory.

In 267 A.D., many buildings were destroyed (the Echo Colonnade, the Metroön, the Leonidaion and others), so as to construct from the rubble a hastily built wall to the south of the Sanctuary, to protect the Temple of Zeus and the chryselephantine statue of the god from the expected invasion by the Herulians. But the invaders did not get as far as Olympia and the Games continued to take place for many years to come. However, at the 262nd Olympiad (269 A.D.), the registers of the Olympic winners stopped. Thereafter there is no more historical information about the Games, nor are there references to the names of Olympic winners, except for the Games of 373 and 385 A.D.

It is evident that the end is approaching.

THE ABOLITION OF THE GAMES

In the Games of 385 A.D., Varazdates the Armenian, afterwards King of the Armenians, won the Boxing. He is also the last known Olympic victor. Eight years later, in 393 A.D., the Olympic Games took place for the last time. The next year (394 A.D.), they were abolished by Theodosius the Great, and a little later (395 A.D.), Pheidias' chryselephantine statue of Zeus was taken to Constantinople.

Thus Olympia was deserted. Christian fanaticism wrought destruction in the deserted Sanctuary in 426 A.D., when Theodosius

II decreed that the Temple of Zeus should be burned. Terrible earthquakes in 522 and 551 A.D. completed the destruction.

During the 5th century A.D., the area was occupied by Christians who built a Byzantine Church on the site of the workshop of Pheidias. Thereafter the erosion of Kronos Hill and flooding by the rivers Alpheios and Kladeos which spilled onto the ruined monuments, gradually covered them with a layer of earth which made them disappear and at the same time protected them for many centuries. In the course of time, even the historical name of Olympia was forgotten and its location was sometimes called Serviana and sometimes Antilalo.

THE EXCAVATIONS

From the beginning of the 18th century antiquarians and archaeologists began to search for the forgotten site of the Olympic Games. In 1723, the French monk Bernard de Montfaucon wrote a letter to Cyrenes, the Archbishop of Corfu, in an unsuccessful attempt to convince him to pursue the exploration of Olympia. Later, in 1767, the German archaeologist Winckelmann intended to secure the permission of the Sublime Porte, in order to excavate the Stadium, but in 1768 he died before managing to realise his objective.

In May 1829, hasty excavations in the Temple of Zeus and the Byzantine Church were made by a French team which, after the Sea Battle of Navarino (1827), followed the expedition of General Maison to the Peloponnese (Expédition Scientifique de Morée). The finds from these excavations — metopes from the opisthodomos of the temple and fragments of metopes from the prodomos — were sent to Paris to adorn the collections in the Louvre.

The first systematic excavations were made between 1875 -1881 by the German Archaeological Institute, funded by the German government. Most of the buildings of the Sanctuary, 130 statues, 6000 coins, 400 inscriptions, many clay objects, 1300 gold and 15,000 bronze objects were found in these excavations at a depth of 5 -7 metres. The same Institute later continued excavations, and also reconstructed part of the Krypte and many columns in the Palaestra and the Temple of Hera. Between 1958-61, the German Institute completed the excavations of the Stadium and up to the present time pursues research on various other monuments in the Sanctuary.

THE REVIVAL OF THE OLYMPIC GAMES

During the 19th century, the rich Olympic tradition preserved in the writing of ancient authors, roused the highest aspirations of the nations of the world for noble contest, fraternization and for peace. So the Olympic Games, which is identified with these great aspirations, became a symbol of modern athletics and contributed decisively to their development.

In the 19th century, many countries of the world, particularly England, Germany and Canada organised athletic galas which were given the imposing name «Olympic Games». In Greece, where the Olympic tradition had profound roots, the first attempt at the revival of the Olympic Games was made in 1838 by the municipality of Pyrgos in Elis, near Olympia, but the outcome is not known. Later Games with the name «Olympic» were established by the E. Zappas Foundation and took place in Athens in 1859, 1870, 1875 and 1887.

All these attempts at the revival of the Olympic Games had a limited national or local character. However, at the end of the 19th century, the French Baron Pierre de Coubertin was inspired with the idea of establishing an International Olympic Games and made the appropriate suggestion to the international congress for athletics, which took place in Paris in 1894. It was proposed that the Olympic Games should take place every four years, as in antiquity, but each time in a different country. They would include in the programme new competitions in addition to the old ones, to ensure the right of athletes from all over the globe to take part regardless of race, class, politics or creed. Finally, thanks to their international character, they would promote peace and cooperation between nations.

Coubertin's suggestion combined in the best manner the competitive traditions of the ancients with the requirements of the modern era. For this reason, it was unanimously decided at the Congress, attended by representatives from thirteen countries, to revive the Olympic Games and at the same time Athens was chosen as the centre for the First International Olympiad. Since then, the Olympic Games are supervised by the International Olympic Committee, which on each occasion appoints a town (not a state), to be responsible for their organisation, following an application by the town. At the same time, the International Olympic Committee cooperates with the National Commitees of the Olympic Games, founded in various countries and so guides the international effort for the development of athletics.

The first International Olympic Games took place in Athens between 5th -15th April, 1896, at the Panathenaikon Stadium. Athletes from thirteen countries took part. The Olympic Hymn, written by the Greek national poet Kostis Palamas and set to music by the Greek composer Spyros Samaras, was instituted at this Olympiad. The Marathon Race (42,000 metres), was also instituted in memory of the heroic Athenian warrior, who on the day of the Battle of Marathon (490 B.C.), brought news of the victory to Athens and then collapsed and died. The race was won by the Greek runner Spyros Louis.

22

After the first Olympiad, which was very successful, the Games took place in 1900 at Paris, in 1904 at St. Louis, in 1908 at London and in 1912 at Stockholm.

The Olympic Flag was chosen by the synod of the International Olympic Committee which took place in 1914 at the French town of Lyons. The flag depicts five coloured, linked circles on a white background. The five circles, which are blue, yellow, black, green and red, symbolise the unity of athletes of the five continents and world brotherhood in general.

In 1916, the Games should have taken place at Berlin, but they were cancelled because the First World War intervened. After the war they took place in 1920 at Antwerp and in 1924 at Paris.

Since 1924, the Winter Olympic Games, which only includes winter sports, has been organised every four years. These Games take place in the winter of the same year in which the Olympics also take place.

In 1928 the Games took place at Amsterdam, in 1932 at Los Angeles and in 1936 at Berlin. At the Olympic Games held in Berlin, the ceremony of the lighting of the Olympic Flame was instituted, as we shall see below.

In 1940 and 1944, the Games were cancelled because of the Second World War. After the war they took place normally in 1948 at London, in 1952 at Helsinki, in 1956 at Melbourne, in 1960 at Rome, in 1964 at Tokyo, in 1968 at Mexico, in 1972 at Munich, in 1976 at Montreal, in 1980 at Moscow. In 1984 they are scheduled to take place at Los Angeles.

In 1961, the International Olympic Committee within the framework of their efforts towards the dissemination of Olympic ideology, founded the International Olympic Academy at Olympia. There, in new buildings, which are near the ancient Stadium, athletes, teachers of gymnastics and others involved with athletics are invited from all over the world to stay and to discuss subjects relating to athletics and the Games.

In the village of ancient Olympia, the Museum of the Modern Olympic Games is under the auspices of the Greek Olympic Games Committee. In this museum rare objects, memorabilia of the modern Olympics, are on exhibition : medals of the Olympic winners, torches used to carry the Olympic Flame from 1936 onwards, Olympic coins, a rich photographic archive, as well as a collection of Olympic stamps, unique in the whole world, which belonged to the founder of the Museum and the great friend of Olympia, G. Papastephanou.

From 1896 until today, the Olympic Games have developed great worldwide authority, have materially served their peaceful aims and are beloved by all the nations of the world. Thus the vision of the Baron Pierre de Coubertin became a reality. Greece, wishing to honour him, raised a monument to him at Olympia. Beside this monument, near the ancient Stadium, at a place named

«The Coubertin Grove», a year after his death, in 1938, was placed his heart preserved in a glass jar. This was the last wish of the great reviver of the Olympic Games.

LIGHTING THE OLYMPIC FLAME

In 1936 the Olympic Games were enhanced by a brilliant ceremony. At the XIth Olympiad, which took place in that year, the Olympic Flame was lit on the sacred site of Olympia and then taken to the Olympic Stadium at Berlin. The ceremony instituted in that year now takes place before each Olympiad, symbolically preserving historical continuity and the sacred links of the Games with the place where they originated, Olympia.

Traditionally, the arrival of the Olympic Flame at the Stadium marks the opening of the Games. Throughout their duration, lasting many days, the flame burns continuously on a huge altar and is only extinguished at the close of the Games.

The lighting of the Olympic Flame takes place on the altar of Hera, which is in front of the Heraion. During the ceremony the altar is surrounded by girls dressed as ancient pristesses, while the Vestal priestess, using a concave mirror made of metal, lights a torch from the rays of the sun and immediately transfers the flame to a krater (a small pottery vase), containing inflammable material. Then all the priestesses form the procession of the dance, which passes through the Krypte, the official entrance into the Stadium. There the Vestal priestess lights a torch from the sacred flame in the krater and hands it to the first runner who runs across the Stadium, in the company of other runners, to the Coubertin Grove, which is in the area of the International Olympic Academy.

The marble altar of the Olympic Flame, made in 1936 for the first such ceremony, has been placed in the Coubertin Grove, beside the monument to Pierre de Coubertin. On reaching the Grove, the first runner lights the marble altar in honour of the man who revived the Olympic Games and afterwards sets off, so beginning the traditional race to Athens.

The flame is always taken to Athens by runners who each go one kilometre. From Athens it is taken to the country for which it is destined sometimes by boat, or by plane, or using lazer beams, so far a unique innovation at the Olympic Games in Montreal, Canada, in 1976. The Olympic Flame has also been carried in the traditional manner over long distances, by thousands of runners each going one kilometre, for example to Berlin (1936), to Munich (1972), and most recently to Moscow (1980).

The Olympic Flame generates feelings of friendship and brotherhood amongst nations and each time rekindles mankind's great aspirations for world peace, the primary object of the International Olympic Games, which is why the flame is always welcomed everywhere with emotional demonstrations and festivities.

THE ARCHAELOGICAL SITE

F ROM THE village at ancient Olympia, a developing tourist centre, (population c. 1000), an asphalt road lined with laurels, cypresses and olive trees, leads the visitor to the archaeological site.

Approaching the site, one meets the bridge over the Kladeos, a rapid winter torrent, which flows past the Sanctuary and a little farther on joins the Alpheios. On the right bank of the river, rising in the west, is a succession of low hills covered with green vegetation, which end up at Dhrouvas Hill.

The Sanctuary is on the right bank of the Alpheios, the most celebrated Peloponnesian river, which spreads out in a fertile valley. Beyond the Alpheios, to the south-east, Mount Lapithis and Mount Tipaion delineate the horizon.

To the north and east, picturesque villages nestle among a series of small hills, planted with pines, which, descending gradually towards the Sanctuary, reach the conical shaped Kronos Hill.

The monuments of Olympia are situated in this extraordinary landscape, between Kronos Hill and the confluence of the Rivers Alpheios and Kladeos.

DESCRIPTION OF THE MONUMENTS

The entrance to the site is next to the bridge over the River Kladeos and near the foot of Kronos Hill, along a steep path which descends to the Sanctuary.

Immediately after entering the Sanctuary, descending 4 to 5 metres below the level of the entrance, one becomes aware of the great depth of deposit removed during excavations which brought these monuments to light. The extent of damage to the monuments is also immediately apparent ; the process of decay began when

25

the games were abolished and was completed by earthquakes in the 6th century A.D.

The monuments described below do not include the ruins of an ancient city, because Olympia was not a city. Olympia was a Sanctuary of Zeus, one of the most important in Greece, and at the same time it was a panhellenic centre for contests, where the most brilliant games in ancient Greece were held. Therefore the buildings erected at various times were intended either for worship or to serve the games.

The buildings used for worship were concentrated round the area of the Sacred Altis. The Altis, which means grove, was densely planted with wild olives, plane trees and other tree species ; it was dedicated to Zeus and the other gods. According to Pausanias, this name had been given to it a long time before. In the Sacred Altis were three temples, dedicated to Zeus, Hera, and Rhea ; the Pelopion ; the Hippodameion ; the Philippeion ; a multitude of altars and thousands of statues.

On the west, a low wall which has two gates (North and South), separated the Altis from a series of buildings which served the athletes, priests and official guests (the Gymnasium, Palaestra, Theokoleon, Leonidaion and others). On the east, the Echo Colonnade separated the Altis from the Stadium.

On the north, behind a wall protecting the Altis from landslides eroding Kronos Hill, were built the Treasuries of ancient Greek cities, while on the south side were the Bouleuterion and the Southern Stoa.

Most of the Sanctuary buildings were constructed using a local fossiliferous limestone, which is mainly derived from the mountains opposite Olympia, parallel to the left bank of the River Alpheios. It is called fossiliferous limestone because it chiefly consists of marine shells. According to geologists, it proves that millions of years ago this area was sea bed.

A visitor's most reasonable query concerns the manner in which the extremely bulky and heavy blocks of stone used for building were lifted into place. Although many theories have been put forward, none of them is universally accepted. Some suggest that by means of soil embankments gradients were made, so that it was much easier to drag the blocks into place. For many reasons this explanation does not seem probable. Others have suggested that lifting devices were used for this purpose. This theory is more widely accepted.

The following description begins with the Gymnasium, sweeps round in a circle as far as the Philippeion and the Prytaneion, and finishes with the most important monument of Olympia, the Temple of Zeus. A plan of the Sanctuary is given on p. 40-41. The numbering of each monument described corresponds to the numbering on this plan, making it easy for the visitor to orientate himself.

I. THE GYMNASIUM

As we enter the site by descending the steep path, the Gymnasium lies on the right. Beside it flows the River Kladeos, which has been responsible for eroding and destroying the whole of the western side of the Gymnasium. The Gymnasium is a large open-air quadrangle, which was surrounded on all four sides by Doric colonnades. Only the ruins of the eastern and southern sides, dating to the 2nd century B.C., survive.

The open quadrangle of the Gymnasium was used by runners and Pentathlon athletes for training. But when weather conditions were unsuitable, during a heat-wave or rain, training took place in the east colonnade (210.51 metres long), as well as in the other three colonnades.

Most of the Gymnasium remains unexcavated. This is apparent when one realises that only an 80 metres long section of the eastern colonnade, which as mentioned above was 210.51 metres long, has been exposed. The rest, which remains buried, extends up to a few metres from the bridge over the Kladeos (towards the new Museum).

2. THE PROPYLON : ENTRANCE TO THE GYMNASIUM

During the Hellenistic period, around 200 B.C., a Corinthian portico (or Propylon), with two internal columns, was built at the south end of the eastern colonnade of the Gymnasium, joining it with the Palaestra. In addition to the lower part of the Propylon, some column drums and capitals survive.

The North Gate to the Altis is situated exactly opposite, to the east; the west wall commences from that point in a southerly direction.

3. THE PALAESTRA

The Palaestra, next to the Gymnasium to the south was built in the 3rd century B.C. It was a square building, sides approximately 66 metres long, with its main entrance at the north-west corner. The lower part of the outer walls were built of stone and the upper part of brick. Inside, was an open square court used by wrestlers, boxers and competitors in the Pankration for training. On the north side of the court, laid out with flat grooved tiles, is a space, measuring 24.20 x 5.44 metres, the purpose of which is unknown.

The court was surrounded by Doric columns. On rainy days or during heat-waves, training took place under cover of the colonnades. Behind the colonnades there were various rooms such as the Elaiothesion where athletes rubbed their bodies with oil, the Konisterion where they dusted themselves with sand, the Ephebeion where they received instruction from trainers, etc. The columns in these rooms are Ionic. At the north-east corner of the court, there is a cistern, 1.40 m. deep, which was used for cold baths.

The German Archaeological Institute partially restored the Palaestra in 1955-6. Total restoration is impossible since many of the columns have been completely destroyed.

4. THE THEOKOLEON

South of the Palaestra is the Theokoleon, where the Theokoloi (priests of Olympia), lived with their assistants. The Theokoloi were in charge of the Sanctuary, sacrifices, and religious observance in general. They were among the few permanent residents of the Sanctuary. Their election from among the important priestly families of Elis, such as that of Iamides or Klytides, took place at each new Olympiad.

The architectural remains of this building show that it was constructed in two periods. The west which had a court surrounded by rooms was built sometime after 350 B.C. The east which had a peristyle court surrounded by rooms dates to the Roman period.

5. THE HEROÖN

West of the Theokoleon is the Heroön. It was built a short time before the Persian Wars. It was a four-sided building and, on its north side, a square walled enclosure surrounded a circular room within which was an altar dedicated to some unknown hero. An inscription found during excavations includes the word «ΗΡΩΟΣ», meaning «of a hero». Following recent research, it is suggested that to begin with it was a hot bath (calderium) and later was converted to the Heroön.

6. BYZANTINE CHURCH — WORKSHOP OF PHEIDIAS

To the south of the Theokoleon and the Heroön is a Byzantine Church. It was built in the style of an Early Christian Basilica, about the mid-5th century A.D., when the area was occupied by Christians. It was constructed on top of an ancient building which was the workshop of Pheidias, where the artist fashioned the chryselephantine statue of Zeus. The workshop was built to the exact dimensions of the cella of the Temple of Zeus, so as to give the artist the same amount of space in which it was intended to place the statue.

28

In recent years during excavations which took place inside and outside the church to the south, moulds which it is believed were used for making the chryselephantine statue of Zeus were found. The moulds were clay models used by Pheidias to shape the gold leaf and make the golden parts of the statue. Tools and chips of ivory were also discovered in the excavation. The finds are discussed in the section on the Museum.

7. THE HOUSE OF THE PHAIDRYNTAI

South of the Byzantine Church are the remains of a building which was probably the House of the Phaidryntai. The Phaidryntai were responsible for taking care of the chryselephantine statue of Zeus and the other statues in the Sanctuary.

8. THE THERMAI

West of the Byzantine Church and the Heroön is a series of ruins which are the Thermai (baths). These date mainly to the Roman period ; some are earlier and date to the Classical period (5th and 4th centuries B.C.). West (towards the Kladeos), was an open-air swimming pool of the 5th century B.C., measuring 24 x 16 metres, which was destroyed during the Ist century B.C. in order to build the baths.

Apart from these baths, the ruins of other complexes of baths dating to the Roman period are located to the west of the Bouleuterion and north of the Prytaneion.

9. THE LEONIDAION

Beyond the House of the Phaidryntai, to the south, is the hostel of the Sanctuary, the Leonidaion. It was built and dedicated to Zeus sometime after 350 B.C., by a wealthy man from Naxos, called Leonidas, after whom it was named.

The Leonidaion was a large two-storey building, measuring 80 x 73.51 metres. On the outside, it was enclosed by a colonnade with 135 Ionic columns. Inside, the open court was surrounded by 44 Doric columns. During the Roman period an ornamental garden and pond with a small island, were laid out in this court. Between the colonnade of the court and the outer colonnade, was a series of rooms used to accomodate distinguished visitors to the Olympic Games.

During the Roman period (Ist and 2nd centuries A.D.), near the Leonidaion and west of the Byzantine Church, two more hostels comprising many rooms and remarkable mosaics were built.

10. THE PROCESSIONAL WAY

The Processional Way is parallel to the western wall of the Altis and lies east of the buildings described above. It is called processional, because the procession of priests, Hellanodikai (umpires), athletes, officials and so on passed along it.

11. THE SOUTH PROCESSIONAL GATE TO THE ALTIS

Opposite the north-east corner of the Leonidaion is the South Processional Gate. The procession entered the Sacred Altis through this gate to go to the Bouleuterion where swearing in took place, or to go to the Great Altar of Zeus where a hecatomb of oxen was sacrificed on the third day of the Games.

12. THE BOULEUTERION

South of the Temple of Zeus is the Bouleuterion, where the Olympic Council met and where official documents and decrees were kept. It was a tripartite building which had on its north and south sides two rectangular sections which ended in apses facing west. The south section had been built during the 6th century B.C. and the north between 490 - 450 B.C. A colonnade with Ionic columns was added to their east side during the Hellenistic period (3rd to 2nd centuries B.C.). Between these two sections is a square, open-air space where the altar of Orkios Zeus, guardian of oaths, and his statue with thunder-bolts in its hands stood. There, after making a sacrifice on the altar, the athletes, Hellanodikai (umpires) and others, took the oath.

In the area between the South Processional Gate to the Altis and the Bouleuterion, there is a multitude of statue bases. Further south are the remains of Roman buildings, the use of which is not known, and also the remains of Roman baths.

13. THE SOUTHERN STOA

The Southern Stoa lies to the south of the Bouleuterion and was built during the 4th century B.C. It was open towards the River Alpheios, with an external colonnade of Doric columns and an internal colonnade of Ionic columns. It was probably used as an agora, or as an official entrance to the Sanctuary. The Sacred Way which started from Elis and ended at the Hippodrome of Olympia, south of the Stadium, passed in front of the Southern Stoa.

30

14. THE TRIUMPHAL ARCH OF NERO

East of the Bouleuterion is Nero's Triumphal Arch, built in 60 A.D. Pausanias does not refer to it. Today only its base survives, showing that it had three openings. On reaching Olympia for the ceremonies of the Olympic Games, the Roman procession passed through this arch to enter the Sacred Altis.

15. THE SOUTH - EAST BUILDING

The South-East Building is situated at the south-east corner of the Altis. It was built in 400 B.C. and was the Sanctuary of the Hestia (Vesta). On top of its foundations and extending to the east, another edifice of brick was built during the Roman period ; it was probably Nero's Villa.

16. THE ECHO COLONNADE

Beyond the South East Building, and to the north, are the ruins of the Echo Colonnade. This colonnade was built during the reign of Philip II of Macedon (about 350 B.C.). It measures 97.81 x 9.81 metres. It had 44 Doric columns on the side of the Altis and an internal colonnade of Ionic columns. The east side was closed by a wall, thus separating the Altis from the Stadium.

It was called the Echo Colonnade because of its extraordinary acoustics. Indeed it is said that it had a sevenfold echo. It was also known by the name Stoa Poikile, because it was decorated with various inscriptions and paintings by famous artists.

In the open space, on the north side of the Echo Colonnade near the entrance to the Stadium, there took place, as was mentioned in the Introduction, competitions for trumpeters and heralds. During the reign of the Emperor Nero, artistic competitions, established by the Emperor himself, also took place there.

In front of the Echo Colonnade is a monument to Ptolemy II of Philadelphos and Arsinoë, his queen (284 - 246 B.C.). On top of the monument's two Ionic columns, measuring 10 metres high, of which only a few column drums now survive, once stood the gold-plated statues of the monarch and his consort.

17. THE KRYPTE

The Krypte lies to the north, beyond the Echo Colonnade, and was the official entrance to the Stadium. It was so named because, during the Ist century B.C., it covered an apse, part of which is reconstructed. In front of the Krypte, on the side of the Altis, was a propylon with Corinthian columns.

18. THE STADIUM

The Stadium lies to the east beyond the Krypte. The German Archaeological Institute which excavated the whole area between 1958 - 61, exposed the track and restored the artificial banks as they were in antiquity.

The track where the athletes competed naked was 192.25 metres, or 600 ancient feet long, by about 30 metres wide. According to tradition the length of the Stadium was fixed by Hercules who measured it with his own feet. The total length of the track, including the margins on its east and west sides, is approximately 212.50 metres.

The starting line was on the east where a series of grooved stone tiles was found. Twenty runners could set off simultaneously from this starting line. Another series of similarly grooved tiles was found on the west side, as one enters the Stadium through the Krypte. This was the finishing line. But for the Diavlos and Dolichos races it was both the starting and the finishing line. In the Diavlos, the runners started from there, ran east, returned in a westerly direction (though not in a circle), to finish at the point from which they had set off. In the Dolichos, this distance was run twelve times (that is 24 times the distance of a Stade race).

An open stone duct with small basins at wide intervals was found all the way around the track in a good state of preservation. The spectators watching the Olympic Games in the parching heat could drink water from it. This water supply system was constructed in 141 - 157 A.D., in conjuction with an aqueduct mentioned later in the description of the Exedra of Herodes Atticus. In earlier days, spectators at the Olympic Games suffered from the lack of water and consequently many died of sun-stroke. Thales, one of the Sages of antiquity, met this fate at Olympia.

The banks of the Stadium, which had no seats, could accomodate 30 - 35,000 spectators. There was a platform on the south bank of the Stadium, near the finishing line, where umpires and officials sat. Opposite the platform, on the north bank, was found the stone altar of Demeter Chamyne. The priestess of Demeter sat on the altar, or on a seat next to it ; of all women, she was the only one permitted to watch the Olympic Games.

The Stadium, in its present form, dates to the 4th century B.C., with alterations made at various times up to the Roman period. It was the third successive stadium built at Olympia. The first, belonging to the Archaic period, lay between the Great Altar of Zeus and the finishing line of today's Stadium ; in the 5th century B.C., the Archaic Stadium was moved to the east until, in the 4th century, the extra space needed in the Sanctuary for an increasing number of dedications and visitors, finally made it necessary to move it to the east. In the resulting free space, new dedications were set up and the Echo Colonnade built which, as has been said, separated the Sacred Altis from the Stadium.

19. THE HIPPODROME

The Hippodrome lay to the south of the Stadium, but was washed away by the Alpheios river, and none of it now remains. It was six stades in length, that is one thousand one hundred and fifty-three metres. The horse and chariot races were held there, the most splendid of all the Olympic events.

20. THE STATUE BASES OF THE ZANES

The Statue Bases of the Zanes stand on the wall to the right, west of the Krypte. The Zanes — plural of Zeus — were sixteen bronze statues of the god, of which only their bases remain. As was mentioned in the Introduction, they were paid for out of the fines which were levied on anyone who broke the rules of the Games, either by offering or accepting bribes to win or lose on purpose. These statues were placed in front of the entrance to the Stadium as a warning.

21. THE TREASURIES

The Treasuries, looking rather like miniature temples, were built in the 6th and 5th centuries B.C. above the retaining wall on top of which are the statue bases for the Zanes. They housed valuable offerings from faithful people and cities, most of them belonging to Greek colonies.

Running from east to west, there are the remains of Treasuries of the following cities : Gela, Megara, Metapontum and Selinus. The owners of the next Treasury are unknown. After that are those of Cyrene, Sybaris, Byzantium, Epidamnus, Syracuse and, lastly, the most magnificent of all, the Sikyonian Treasury.

According to Wilhelm Dörpfeld, after the Sikyonian Treasury was the Idaean Cave and the altar of Idaean Hercules. To the north, next to the semicircular Exedra of Herodes Atticus, was the small temple of Eileithyia and Sosipolis. Eileithyia was the goddess of childbirth, and Sosipolis, her son. According to local tradition, once, when the Arcadians were invading Elis, Eileithyia appeared and gave her infant son to the Eleian army, whereupon, having transformed himself into a dragon, he put the enemy to flight and saved the city, hence his name (Saviour of the City).

22. THE METROÖN

Below the Sikyonian Treasury lies the Metroön, a temple sacred to the Mother of the Gods, Rhea or Kybele. Built between 400 and 360 B.C., it has eleven Doric columns along each side, and six at either end. It measures 20.67 m. by 10.62 m., and was about 7.50 m. high. In Roman times, it housed statues of Roman Emperors, including a huge one of Octavian Augustus, now in the old Museum, which was set up in the cella of the temple. Somewhere, a few metres to the west of the opisthodomos of the temple, was the Altar of Rhea.

23. THE EXEDRA OF HERODES ATTICUS

The Exedra of Herodes Atticus stands to the west of the Treasuries. Herodes Atticus was a philosopher and orator from Marathon who built the aqueduct of the Sanctuary at his own expense between 141 and 157 A.D. The water, which was particularly valuable for the host of pilgrims during the Games, was brought from a spot three kilometres east of the Sanctuary, where there is still a spring today. Originally it was collected in a semicircular reservoir high up, from which it flowed through lion-head spouts to a long and narrow reservoir at a lower level, and, thence, was chanelled through pipes to the Stadium or wherever it was needed.

The long narrow reservoir was decked out at its two ends with circular peristyles, one of which (to the west) has been partially restored. Statues of the family of Herodes Atticus and of Romans were set up on the upper part, on the semi-circular storage tank, while in the middle, in front of the pool, a statue of bull was erected which is now in the Museum.

24. THE PREHISTORIC BUILDINGS

Below the Exedra of Herodes Atticus to the south, there are the remains of two prehistoric buildings about one metre beneath present ground level, which were excavated by Dörpfeld. They date to between 2000 and 1500 B.C. and, together with the other prehistoric remains, illustrate the antiquity of settlement in the Sanctuary area.

25. THE TEMPLE OF HERA

The Heraion or Temple of Hera, lies to the west of the prehistoric buildings and is one of the oldest temples in Greece. It was built around 600 B.C. and has six columns of the Doric order at either end and sixteen along each side. The temple measures 50 m.

by 18.75 m. and was about 7.80 m. high. The upper parts of the walls were of mud-brick built on a socle of fossiliferous limestone. The original columns were of wood but were later replaced, at different times, by limestone ones. Thus, although all are of the Doric order, each differs in details of the capital, the fluting and the basic proportions. It is worth noting that Pausanias, around 160 A.D., saw one wooden column in the opisthodomos of the temple.

The prodomos, at the east of the temple, had two columns at the front. Next is the cella, where two rows of columns, on the right and left divided the temple into three parts. Between every second column and the walls of the temple were small partition walls forming rectangular niches which used to hold various statues. The Hermes of Praxitiles was housed in the second niche on the right where it was found during the excavation of the temple. The cult statue of the goddess Hera, enthroned, was placed at the far end of the cella ; and next to it was a statue of Zeus, standing upright dressed as a warrior. Sadly, only the head of Hera now remains from these two statues, now in the Museum.

The opisthodomos of the temple, at the western end, is separated from the cella by a wall. Like the prodomos, it had two columns at the front. Various sacred and valuable things were kept safe here, such as the chryselephantine table for the victors' wreaths, made by Pheidias' apprentice Kolotis, and the chest of Kypselos engraved with a number of mythological scenes.

The Altar of Hera, where the Olympic flame is lit today, is to the east of the Heraion.

The German Archaeological Institute has restored four columns of the temple, two quite recently, and the Greek Archaeological Service has restored the huge circular central akroterion of the temple, which is now on display in the Museum.

26. THE PRYTANEION

North-west of the Heraion are the remains of the Prytaneion where the celebratory feasts, in honour of the winners and official guests, were held during the Games.

The architectural remains of the building show that it must have been built towards the end of the 6th century B.C., and that, at times — particularly during the Roman period, as is demonstrated by the brick walls — it was reconstructed and extended, so much so that it almost lost its original form.

The Altar of Hestia (Vesta) was in the Prytaneion, on which the «eternal flame» burnt night and day. Each year, the Olympian Priests, following tradition, would make a clayey mixture from the ashes of the altar mixed with water from the Alpheios, and daub the Great Altar of Zeus with it. The altar of the goddess Hestia seems to have been in the square room on the southern side of the

Prytaneion. The rooms to the west and the peristyle court to the north, were used for feasting and cooking.

27. THE PHILIPPEION

The Philippeion is to the west of the Heraion. It seems that it was begun during the reign of Philip II of Macedon, most probably after the battle of Chaeronea (338 B.C.) and completed, after Philip's death (336 B.C.) by his son Alexander the Great who honoured his father by naming it after him.

The building is circular with a diameter of 15.24 m. and was surrounded by eighteen Ionic columns. It had a conical roof with marble tiles and antefixes. Inside the circle of columns was a circular wall, with an entrance from the south-east, forming a room which housed the gold and ivory statues of Philip, his wife, Olympias, his parents, Amyntas and Eurydike, and his son, Alexander. All stood on a semi-circular pedestal. Leochares was the sculptor.

The Philippeion has suffered great damage. Of this elegant building, only the lower parts, fragments of the architrave, roof panels, tiles and capitals, now remain.

28. THE PELOPION

To the south of the Heraion, in the direction of the opisthodomos of the Temple of Zeus, lies the Pelopion which dates c. 1100 B.C. This was a low mound, originally surrounded by a circular wall, which was the cenotaph of the local hero, Pelops. In the 6th. century B.C., a pentagonal wall replaced the circular one, having an entrance and propylon on the south-west side. Each year, a black ram was sacrificed on the cenotaph in honour of Pelops.

The Hippodameion was the equivalent monument dedicated to Pelops' wife, Hippodameia who was honoured each year with sacrifices in an all female ritual. Although no traces of this building have been found in the course of excavations, contemporary scholars placed it to the west of the Temple of Zeus.

29. THE HOUSE OF OINOMAOS

Pausanias tells us that, between the Great Altar and the Temple of Zeus, was a column, under shelter, from the ancient palace of Oinomaos, King of Pisa, which was destroyed by a thunderbolt sent by Zeus. An inscription read as follows : *I am what is left of the famous house, traveller, I have been a pillar in the halls of Oinomaos ; am now with Zeus, son of Kronos, holding chains ; and am venerable : dreadful flaming fire has not destroyed me.* (*Pausanias V,20,7* — Translated by P. Levi, S. J. —1971, Penguin).

30. THE GREAT ALTAR OF ZEUS

The Great Altar of Zeus was situated in the area between the three temples of Zeus, Hera and Rhea, but has not survived. Great sacrifices were made on it during the Games. It was about seven metres high but became higher as the deposit of ashes became deeper and as more of the clayey mixture, referred to in connection with the Prytaneion, was daubed onto it. The great height of the Altar allowed thousands of worshippers to watch the sacrifices from the surrounding area.

Apart from the Great Altar of Zeus, there were sixty-nine other altars in the Sanctuary dedicated to various gods, where the Theokoloi sacrificed, following a strict order.

31. THE TEMPLE OF ZEUS

In the very centre of the Altis are the ruins of the Temple of Zeus. This temple, a model of harmony and symmetry, was the work of the Eleian architect Livon, and turned out to be the most splendid building in the Sanctuary of Olympia. Built on top of a stepped platform which gave it greater height, its spectacular presence commanded the surrounding area as was fitting for the house of the supreme god of the Greeks.

The construction of the temple was carried out between 470 and 456 B.C., paid for with the spoils of the war between the Eleians and Pisans in 472 B.C. which ended in the destruction of Pisa, as has been mentioned above.

The indisputable date for the construction of the temple (470 - 456 B.C.) raises a question. Was there a temple dedicated to Zeus in the Sanctuary before 470 B.C.? And next, how can one explain the dedication of a temple to Hera in 600 B.C. in the Sanctuary of Zeus but not of one to Zeus himself ?

There are two schools of thought concerning this problem. One would have another Temple of Zeus until 470 B.C. when the new one was built. The other, now generally thought to be correct, suggests that the Temple of Hera served as a joint building for both Hera and Zeus until 470 B.C. This theory gains more weight when one remembers that a statue of Zeus stood next to that of Hera in the Heraion.

The chief building material was local fossiliferous limestone often stuccoed with white marble dust. The roof tiles, the gargoyles and the sculptures for the Temple were made of Parian marble, later reconstructions using Pentelic marble.

The temple was a Doric peripteral building (6 by 13 columns) measuring 64.12 m. by 27.66 m. and 20.25 m. high. The columns themselves were about 10.45 m. high with a diameter at the base of 2.20 m. and were connected by a heavy epistyle (lintel) on top of which rested the triglyphs and metopes. The metopes were not originally decorated. But, in 146 B.C., twenty-one were adorned each with a golden shield (ten on the east side and eleven on the south) dedications of the Roman General Mummius from the spoils of his victories over the Achaeans. The pediments of the temple (i.e. the two triangles, one at either end of the building above the metopes and triglyphs) were decked out with sculptures which are now in the Museum.

In the middle of the eastern end was a ramp which is still extant. Entering from there, one comes to the prodomos. Before the entrance of the prodromos, on the right, there is a small area which was paved in the Roman era with coloured hexagonal tiles. There, during the Games, they used to bring the chryselephantine table, normally kept in the Heraion, which was used for the wild olive wreaths ; it was the work of Pheidias' apprentice Kolotis. The crowning of the Olympic victors, happened on the last day of the Games, at the entrance to the temple, and was watched by the crowd from the surrounding area.

At the entrance to the prodomos, between the pillasters, were two Doric columns — smaller than those outside — supporting a frieze of triglyphs and metopes. The metopes were sculptured with scenes from the Labours of Hercules, now in the Museum. On the floor of the prodomos are the remains of a Hellenistic mosaic showing Tritons.

The cella is in the middle of the temple connected with the prodomos by a passage 4.80 m. wide. It was enclosed by a wall on its north, south and west sides. Inside the cella were two colonnades of seven Doric columns parallel to the north and south walls, the lower parts of which still remain. The columns supported a second tier, so forming a gallery. Worshippers could climb up there by means of a wooden staircase to marvel at the chryselephantine statue of Zeus. The great work of Pheidias stood at the far end of the cella between the two colonnades and was isolated from the surrounding area by a railing cordoning off the pedestal and the greater part of the floor in front. This floor, made of Eleusinian marble, a little of which still remains, would be covered in oil which had been poured over the statue to protect the ivory from damp.

At the western end, a wall separated the cella from the opisthodomos which, like the prodomos, had two Doric columns at its entrance, which supported a frieze of triglyphs and metopes. The latter also showed scenes from the Labours of Hercules, now in the Museum. In front of the entrance of the opisthodomos was the Bema (rostrum) from which, as mentioned above, famous men of the Ancient Greece have addressed the Greeks.

The Temple of Zeus, the most splendid building in the Altis, has been damaged many times. As we have said, it was burnt down in 426 A.D. on the orders of Theodosius II. Later, in 522 and 551, earthquakes destroyed it and many other buldings, as the fallen columns on the south side show. Not one column stands to-day, while architectural fragments lie all around.

*

The area round the temple is scattered with statue bases — main-ly of gods, heroes and Olympic victors — dedicated by cities or individuals. Amongst these, a short distance from the south-east corner of the temple, the triangular base of the Nike of Paionios is noticeable. The statue itself, and part of the base, are now in the Museum.

Note also that, near the west side of the temple, was the altar of the Kallistephanos Nymphs next to which grew the sacred wild olive from which branches for the victory wreaths were cut.

THE CHRYSELEPHANTINE STATUE OF ZEUS

With the chryselephantine statue of Zeus, not only did Pheidias surpass the achievement of his statue of Athena Parthenos, but al-so revealed the true god of the Ancients Greeks as they believed him to be and as he, himself, lived in their minds.

The statue was made sometime after 432 B.C., since, about that time, Pheidias was accused and convicted by the Athenians of em-bezelling the gold for the statue of Athena. The Eleians then asked him to undertake this great work. To this end, he built his workshop in Olympia, as has been said, and probably remained there for the rest of his life.

Although nothing remains of the statue, it is known from va-rious sources that it was seven times larger than life, and, together with the base, stood about 12.40 m. high. Zeus was seated on his splendid throne, and, according to Strabo, if he were to have stood up, he would have burst through the roof of the temple. In his right hand he held a gold and ivory Nike, and in his left, a sceptre made of all the metals known at that time. An eagle surmounted the sceptre, symbolizing the power of the god.

The craftsman had skilfully fixed ivory and gold sheets into the wooden frame of the statue. The bare parts of the body — those parts not covered by the robe, namely, the face, the arms and the feet — were made of ivory. The robe itself, adorned with signs of the zodiac and lilies, the sandals, the beard and the hair were all made of gold, while his head was crowned with a silver olive wreath. The throne was made of bronze, ebony, gold, ivory and precious stones. The apprentices of Pheidias, Panainos and Kolo-tis, decorated it with a host of mythological scenes.

In Greek mythology, Zeus was a formidable god, both judge and castigator, always ready to hurl his thunderbolt. Nevertheless, he was the «Kindly One» who was sympathetic to human wea-kness and protecting good.

39

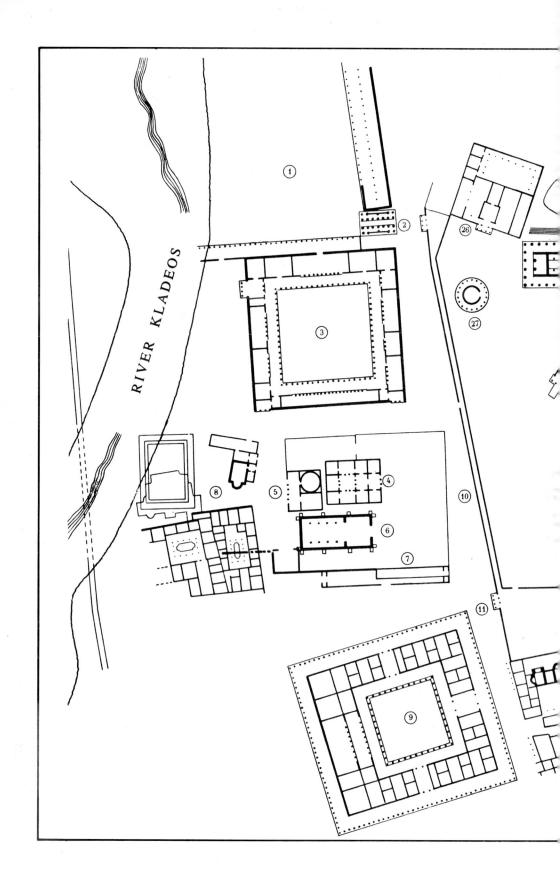

RIVER KLADEOS

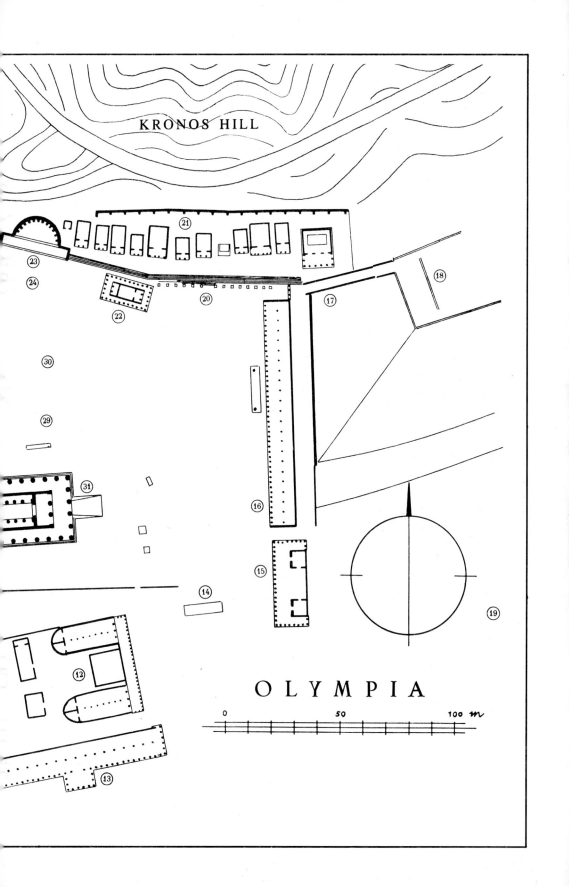

KRONOS HILL

OLYMPIA

0   50   100 m

The Zeus of Pheidias was the «Kindly One», the good god full of love and sympathy for man. His face bore an expression of infinite calm, Olympian serenity, graciousness and gentleness. With these features, the great craftsman portrayed Zeus in his supreme glory, just as he was conceived in the imagination of the Greeks.

The success with which the divine form was portrayed aptly inspired the poet, Philip of Salonika to write the following epigram :

Either God came down from Heaven to show you his image,
Pheidias, or you went to see God.

Dion Crysostome, wrote : *If a man, with a heavily burdened heart, who has drunk the cup of grief and sorrow in life and whom sweet sleep visits no more, happens to stand before the statue, he will forget the wretched things which afflict a man's life.*

This masterpiece of Pheidias was the first of the seven Wonders of the World, and became the centre of everyone's admiration as no other work had before. Arrian confirms this when he tells us that it was thought a great shame for anyone to die before seeing the chryselephantine statue of Zeus.

After which, it may seem somewhat paradoxical when Strabo refers to the occasion when Panainos asked Pheidias whence came his inspiration for the face of Zeus, and Pheidias replied by quoting the following lines from the Iliad :

The son of Kronos spake, and bowed his dark brow in assent,
and the ambrosial locks waved from the king's immortal head ;
and he made great Olympus to quake.

(*Iliad I: 528-530* — Translated by A.T. Murray-1960, Loeb).

These lines, however, are a very long way from the peaceful and serene Zeus of Pheidias.

Pausanias tells us that, according to legend, when Pheidias completed the work, he asked Zeus to send him a sign to indicate whether he approved of it or not. So, the god immediately approved and hurled a thunderbolt at the temple withour destroying anything. A bronze hydria was placed next to the statue on the spot where the thunderbolt had struck.

In the Roman period, Emperor Caligula (37 - 41 A.D.) wanted the statue to be brought to Rome. There, he planned to replace the head with a copy of his own. However, this failed because, according to tradition, either the ship which was entrusted with the task sank on the way, or, «when certain men went in to take the statue, it roared with laughter and they fled».

The statue stood in situ until 393 A.D., a little time after which (395 A.D.) it was carried off to Constantinople, where, according to the historians Kedrinos and Zonaras, it perished in the great fire of 475 A.D.

THE ARCHAELOGICAL MUSEUM

T HE NEW Museum of Olympia was built recently, near the archaeological site, in a shady grove beneath the northern slope of Kronos Hill. The arcaeological finds which used to be in the old Museum and the most important finds from recent excavations are displayed in the spacious galleries of this simple modern building.

In 1886, the old Museum was built on the low pine-covered hill, a little beyond the bridge over the Kladeos, very near the village at Ancient Olympia. Somewhere near the old Museum was the grave of King Oinomaos of Pisa, which according to Pausanias (VI, 21, 3) *«is a mound of earth surrounded by a stone wall, and above the grave there are ruined buildings where they say he stabled his mares»*.

The transfer of exhibits from the old to the new Museum is almost complete. However, in the old Museum it is still possible to see the plaster casts of the two pediments of the Temple of Zeus, and some exhibits (such as the Nike of Paionios, Octavian Augustus etc.), which have not yet been transferred to the new Museum.

In the new Museum the description of exhibits follows the order in which the galleries are numbered on the plan (p. 44). For practical reasons, the exhibits in the Central Gallery are described last, since the visitor will find it easier to look at the other galleries first.

GALLERY I

The visitor on entering the Museum comes to the first gallery, where there are several 5th century B.C. inscribed statue bases. There is also a new model of the Sanctuary of Olympia as reconstructed by the German Archaeological Institute. In the old

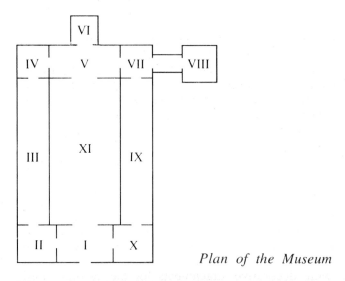

Plan of the Museum

Museum, another model of the Sanctuary made by the German architect Hans Schleif in 1931, is based on a drawing by Wilhelm Dörpfeld. Both models are useful because they help the visitor to get an idea of the original appearance of the Sanctuary.

GALLERY II

In the second Gallery, to the left of the Museum entrance, the cases contain important finds of the prehistoric period, from the Sanctuary and surrounding area.

The earliest finds are some small stone tools, clay vases and sherds of the Late Neolithic period (c. 4000 - 3000 B.C.), as well as whole pots and sherds of the Early Helladic and Middle Helladic periods (E.H. c. 2800 - 1900 B.C.; M.H. c. 1900 - 1600 B.C.). These were found at various times in the Stadium, the Altis and in the area of the new Museum.

Amongst the earliest finds are three marble Cycladic figurines of the 3rd millenium B.C., which were found at the village of Neraidha in the Nome of Elis, and in the area of Pheia, a submerged ancient city in the bay of Aghios Andreas, near the port of Katakolo.

Most of the cases contain vases, jewellery and various other artefacts of the Mycenaean period (c. 1600 - 1100 B.C.), the majority being Late Mycenaean (c. 1425 - 1100 B.C.). These finds, with their remarkably preserved colours, come from chamber tombs in the area of the new Museum and the district around Ancient Olympia : Kladeos, Makrisia, Dhiasela (Broumazi), Samikon etc.

Finds from the Sanctuary of Olympia, dating to the Geometric period (c. 900 - 700 B.C.) are also on display in this gallery. During the Geometric period, so called because of the typical geo-

44

metrical designs on the pottery, the Sanctuary of Olympia received many votives, or thanksgiving offerings, to Zeus. The most splendid of these are the bronze tripod cauldrons, which were usually elaborately decorated. Noteworthy too are the clay, and particularly the bronze figurines offered on their own as votives, or as part of tripod cauldrons to which they were attached as decoration.

There are two bronze tripods in this gallery. The one on the left as we enter, dating to the end of the 8th century B.C., is very elegant. The other, which is opposite, is the oldest tripod of the Geometric period (9th century B.C.), and is very well preserved.

In the case on the right as we enter the gallery, a whole series of bronze tripod feet with elaborate linear decoration, dating from the 9th to the end of the 8th centuries B.C., are on display. The oldest of these are cast solid, while the later ones are cast or hammered. Next to this, in a small case are bronze kouroi (young men), which were decorative attachments for the handles of tripod cauldrons of the 7th century B.C. These are reconstructed in the drawing beside them.

The next case contains a large number of clay and bronze objects of the 9th and 8th centuries B.C., mainly animal and human figurines, chariots with charioteers, miniature tripods, tripod handles etc.

Finally, cordoned off in the middle of the gallery, is a magnificent horse of solid bronze which is considered unique for its large size. This piece dates to the Late Geometric period (760 - 700 B.C.).

GALLERY III

In the next gallery are finds from the Sanctuary at Olympia, which date from the end of the Geometric period (8th century B.C.), to the Archaic period (7th and 6th centuries B.C.). During those centuries apart from cauldrons and figurines, numerous weapons, the offerings of warriors and victors or the spoils of war, were dedicated to the Sanctuary.

In the case to the left of the entrance, there are clay and bronze, human and animal figurines, groups representing hunting scenes, and various other small finds of the 8th century B.C. These were either single votives or the decorative attachments of tripod handles. These continue the exhibits of the Geometric period in the previous gallery.

In a case on our right, numerous protomes of lions, griffins and sirens are on display. These were decorations attached to tripod rims and date from the end of the 8th to the beginning of the 6th centuries B.C. The huge cauldrons in the gallery, belonging to the same period, were adorned with similar protomes. It is worth no-   45

ting that these motifs (lions, griffins, sirens etc.), are of oriental origin. Their appearance in the Greek world is due to a profo-
und Oriental influence on Hellenic art during the 7th century
B.C.; hence the term «Orientalizing» for the art of this period.

On the left as we enter the gallery, three hammered sheet bronzes are examples of oriental art. Made at the end of the 8th
century B.C., in a Near Eastern workshop, bearing Assyrian representations, they probably formed the three-sided base of a vessel.

*

There are also in this gallery, many ornate bronze plaques of
the Archaic period (7th and 6th centuries B.C.), used to cover
shields, wooden chests and other objects.

On the right hand side of the gallery, there are plaques on which one can distinguish fascinating scenes like that of a warrior de-
parting for battle saying farewell to his family (c. 590 B.C.) ;
that of Theseus abducting Antiope and of Orestes killing his mother, Clytemnestra (c. 570 B.C.) ; that of lion devouring a deer
(c. 670 B.C.), etc.

On the left, amongst the rest, there are two more interesting
plaques. One (c. 620 B.C.), probably served as the covering of
the metope of a temple and depicts a female griffin suckling her
newborn. The other (c. 630 B.C.) represents two centaurs battering
Caeneus King of the Lapiths, with the trunks of fir-trees, to drive
him into the earth and so destroy him, since according to legend,
Caeneus was immortal and there was no other way of killing him.

Bronze plaques with various representations, mainly mythological, used as devices adorning the centre of shields, were freq-
uently found in the Sanctuary. Some of these are on show, such as
the one, on the left hand side, depicting a dreadful face, probably
that of Phobos (Fear), and the one on the right, depicting the
winged Gorgon (both 6th century B.C.).

*

As already mentioned, during the Archaic period (7th and 6th
centuries B.C.), weapons were frequent offerings at the Sanctuary
of Olympia. Excavations have revealed a multitude of shields, helmets, breast-plates, greaves, arrowheads, spears etc., part of which is exhibited in this gallery.

On the left and right hand walls are large shields and breast-plates
in remarkably good condition.

There are two important breast-plates on show in a special case
in the centre of the gallery. One dates after the mid-7th century
B.C. and is engraved on the upper half with lions, bulls, sphinxes
and panthers, while below, Zeus and Apollo are depicted with

other gods and goddesses in the background. It was found before 1870 at Olympia in the bed of the Alpheios River, but was sent abroad during the 2nd World War. Then in 1969, it was auctioned in Switzerland at a sale of antiquities, at which it was bought by the PSYCHAS Foundation which donated it to the Museum. On the other (c. 670 B.C.), at the back of the case, is an engraving of the Dioskouroi freeing their sister Helen after she had been kidnapped by Theseus and Peirithous. Drawings of the breast-plates and their decoration are next to the case on the wall.

A great variety of intricately decorated helmets, arm-guards, forearm guards, belts, thigh-pieces, greaves, ankle-guards and foot-guards, which make up the complete bronze armour of the Archaic hoplite are on display.

A series of Corinthian-type helmets in the right hand case, illustrate their development from the end of the 8th century to the middle of the 5th century B.C.

In another case, further on, Illyrian-type helmets, spanning the 8th to the mid-6th centuries B.C. are shown along with greaves, belts, thigh-pieces, ankle-guards, foot-guards, spearheads, arrow-heads etc.

Next, in a separate case, is an Illyrian, bronze helmet (c. 530 B.C.), with inlaid silver decoration ; on the front, a boar is flanked by two lions and on each cheek piece there is a horseman.

To the left, a case with spearheads and arrowheads, and a series of greaves illustrate the development of these types from the Geometric period to the middle of the 5th century B.C.

Finally in a case further on, there are helmets, greaves, thigh-pieces, arm-guards, etc., while next to it is a numbered illustration of every part of the armour of a hoplite of the Archaic period.

*

During the Archaic period, figurines, usually of bronze, continued to be valuable votive gifts to the Sanctuary. After the weaponry, on the left and right of the gallery, are many figurines, single votives or tripod attachments, representing gods, heroes, victorious warriors, runners, charioteers and animals, mainly horses and griffins.

In the centre of the gallery, to the left, there is a remarkable 6th century B.C. statue of hammered bronze. It represents a mythical beast with one wing and has eyes of inlaid bone. This statue is an example of the method which was used during the Archaic period to make big bronze statues. In the mid-6th century B.C. a new method was discovered which thereafter enabled craftsmen to cast large statues because they were hollow. This is called the lost wax process («cire perdu»). The invention of this new method is attributed by ancient Greek tradition to the Samian craftsmen Rhoikos and Theodoros.

*

In addition to the bronzes, there are several other important finds. At the far end of the gallery to the left, there is a lion's head sculptured from limestone, which was probably a fountain head ; it dates to the mid-7th century B.C. Opposite it, on the right, is a colossal 6th century B.C. head, also of limestone, from a cult statue of Hera which, as already mentioned, stood in the temple dedicated to the goddess. It is outstanding for the Archaic smile, a feature which appears for the first time and from then on prevails on the Archaic statues of Kouroi (young men), and Korai (young women).

Dominating the far end of the gallery, is a huge painted terracotta akroterion (late 7th century B.C.), from the apex of the pediment of the Temple of Hera ; it has been admirably restored by the Greek Archaeological Service and beside it is a drawn reconstruction. Behind this exhibit there are two terracotta antefixes also from the Temple of Hera.

To the right of the exit is a Kouros (c. 570 B.C.), found at Phygalia, while to the left of the exit is a piece of a remarkable terracotta akroterion (6th century B.C.), from an unknown building, possibly a Treasury. It is reconstructed in a drawing next to the exhibit.

GALLERY IV

This gallery contains finds of the Archaic period (7th and 6th centuries B.C.), including single votive offerings, decorative attachments of different types of vessel, and decorations from various buildings in the Sanctuary.

There are many painted vases in this gallery, so well preserved that they might have been painted yesterday. There are also clay house models, terracotta figurines and other objects.

In the last case on the left, is an exquisite head of a woman (c. 520 B.C.), part of a terracotta statue, which probably adorned the pediment of the Treasury of Sybaris.

Other cases contain numerous bronzes, such as beautifully modelled figurines, the feet and handles of tripod cauldrons and various other impressively decorated vessels, vases and utensils etc.

On the right, there is a marble statue of a veiled woman standing on a lion (late 7th century B.C.), only part of which was recovered. This compositon together with two similar ones, which have not been found, supported a perirranterion or basin which was used to cleanse the hands during a libation. To the left is a

48

late 7th century B.C., earthenware perirranterion with relief decoration, found at Skillounta (Babes).

At the end of the gallery, opposite the entrance, is the pediment of the Treasury of the Megarians (late 6th century B.C.). It is made of porous limestone and depicts the battle between the gods and giants. It is reconstructed in the drawing beside it.

Clay decorations from the Sanctuary buildings are also on display here. Pieces which have survived, mainly terracotta antefixes and gutters from the Archaic buildings of the Altis, are decorated with elaborate designs and preserve their original colours. There is also part of a clay attachment of the pediment of the Treasury of the Geloans (6th century B.C.).

To the left of the exit from this gallery, there is a bronze battering ram, dating to the mid-5th century B.C.

GALLERY V

Finds of the Early Classical period (480 - 445 B.C.), and Classical period (5th and 4th centuries B.C.) :

To the left of the entrance, is a rare terracotta statue, admirably preserved, which was found in the Stadium. It represents the Rape of Ganymede by Zeus. The cock held by Ganymede was a symbol of love for the ancient Greeks and it indicates that the beautiful boy was Zeus' favourite. According to another legend, Ganymede the son of Troos or Laomedon became a cup-bearer to the gods. The statue, which was made around 470 B.C., was probably a central akroterion for the adornment of a building in the Altis.

Another rare terracotta statue (c. 490 B.C.), also found in the Stadium, is in the last case on the left. It may represent a warrior (?) and is most probably a decoration from a pediment of a building in the Altis.

Among the other terracotta statues in this gallery, one should note, to the left of the entrance, a lion couchant (second half of the 5th century B.C.), and to the right, a dolphin (c. 400 B.C.), which was probably an akroterion. In the first display case on the right, is a splendid head of Athena from a terracotta statue (c. 490 B.C.), and a kore and satyr group (c. 500 B.C.), which was probably the akroterion of a Treasury. There is a reconstruction in the drawing next to the group.

In the case on the right there are some exquisitely made bronze statuettes of gods, animals, birds etc., the feet of bronze statues and bronze locks of statues etc. Among the most impressive of these priceless works are : a small bronze horse (c. 470 B.C.), the only one surviving from a four-horse chariot ; a small, very elegant, bronze eagle (5th century B.C.) ; the ear and horn of a huge bronze bull (the pedestal was found at the north-eastern side of the Temple of Zeus), which the Eretrians had dedicated in the

49

Altis to commemorate their victory over the Athenians in the early 5th century B.C. ; and, lastly, the bronze handle of a vessel which depicts two lions devouring a deer (c. 480 B.C.).

In the next case are finds from the workshop of Pheidias, found in a bank of earth, in an area to the south of the workshop. The finds include : terracotta moulds which the great artist used to cast the gold parts of the gold and ivory statue of Zeus ; fragments of ivory ; bone tools ; obsidian ; anthemium leaves of glass ; fragments of sheet bronze ; the sherds of a krater painted by the artist Cleophon (440 - 430 B.C.) ; a goldsmith's small hammer and anvil and so on. The most fascinating object, however, is a small oinochoë which was one of Pheidias personal belongings. It has the following inscription on its base : *ΦΕΙΔΙΟ ΕΙΜΙ* meaning *«I belong to Pheidias»*.

In the last case on the right there is an important series of iron objects, used in everyday life in the Classical period, including agricultural digging tools, cutting implements, spits etc.

In the cases on the left, there are several helmets of historical importance. One of these probably belonged to Miltiades, the Athenian general who in 490 B.C. led the victory against the Persians at Marathon. It is probable that after the battle the general dedicated his helmet to Zeus. On the helmet's left cheek-piece there is an inscription : *Miltiades presented this to Zeus*. In the same case is a Persian helmet taken as booty in one of the battles against the Persians during the early 5th century B.C. The Athenians dedicated it to Zeus ; it bears the inscription : *To Zeus from the Athenians, who took it from the Medes*.

Two more bronze helmets one Corinthian and the other Etruscan, were dedicated to Zeus by Hieron, tyrant of Syracuse and the Syracusans after their victory in 474 B.C., over the Tyrrhenians (Etruscans) at Cyme, South Italy. They each bear the same inscription, engraved on the left side. It is worth noting that there is another Etruscan helmet, in the British Museum, which bears the same inscription.

In this gallery there are also some remarkable marble statues of the gods, particularly Zeus, which are Hellenistic copies of bronze statues by famous 5th century B.C. artists such as Polykleitos among others.

GALLERY VI

THE NIKE OF PAIONIOS

This gallery will remain closed until the statue is transferred from the old Museum, where it is still on exhibition.

The statue of Nike is one of the most interesting works representing the Classical style. It was made sometime between 425 and 421 B.C. out of marble, by the famous sculptor Paionios of Mende in the Chalkidike, and is inscribed with his name. The same artist executed the eastern akroteria of the Temple of Zeus.

The inscription tells us that the statue was dedicated by the Messenians and Naupactians as one tenth of their spoils of war, in gratitude for their victory over the Spartans at Sphacteria in 425 B.C., during the Peloponnesian War. The inscription reads as follows :

> *Messenians and Naupactians dedicate to Olympian*
> *Zeus one tenth of the spoils of war.*
> *Paionios of Mende made it*
> *and also the akroteria of the temple...*

The statue, as already mentioned, was set up a short distance from the south-east corner of the Temple of Zeus. It was about 3 metres high and stood on a 9 metres high triangular pedestal comprising 12 drums. The pedestal, the great height of the statue leaning forward with the weight on the left foot, and the outstretched wings, now only fragmentary, gave the impression of the Nike descending from the heavens to crown the victors with the olive wreath which she held in her right hand. Her raised left hand clasps her diaphanous doric peplos, which billowed out behind her clinging to her shapely body. This impetuous movement uncovers her left leg and shoulder up to the breasts. At her back is the peplos in a mass of elegant folds, Under her right foot is the head of an eagle with inlaid wings, showing that the goddess is descending from great heights.

By making the body lean forward, the artist has cleverly given his work a feeling of continual and harmonious motion and grace. The forward movement is counterbalanced by the backward billowing of the peplos which hides the real stabilising force, namely the trunk. In this original way Paionios fixed the statue to its base. Hence the visitor is attracted to the Nike of Paionios, not only by its exquisite beauty, but also by the unique technical achievement in the way it is balanced.

GALLERY VII

Finds from the Sanctuary of Olympia and Ancient Elis, Pyrgos etc. (Late 4th to 2nd centuries B.C.) :

The case on the right contains vases and a set of figurines, mainly female, hands of bronze statues etc. On the left is a case exhibiting heads from female marble statuettes, small vases and other objects.

Of particular interest in this gallery are the the following : a head of Alexander the Great (a copy of a Lysippus statue), found

51

near the village of Alpheiousa near Olympia ; the head of an athlete of the Hellenistic period ; the base of a bronze statue of an athlete of which only the foot survives (3rd century B.C.) ; a lion tearing a ram to pieces, found in the village of Varvarsaina near Olympia (4th century B.C.) ; a bronze head of a child found in the Stadium (Hellenistic) and next to it a pewter reproduction ; a marble statue probably of Dionysus (early 4th century B.C.), etc.

Lastly, high up on the left, there is a series of 4th century B.C. painted terracotta lion heads, which were gargoyles of the inner court of the Leonidaion.

GALLERY VIII

THE HERMES OF PRAXITELES

One of the best known works of the 4th century B.C. stands in this gallery, namely the Hermes of Praxiteles. In that century, Praxiteles and Skopas stand apart from even the most renowned Greek artisans. Praxiteles concerned himself with physical beauty, portraying human charm and compassion, whereas Skopas was more interested in expressing character with extreme pathos and suffering.

The Hermes, while not being one of his best works, is very graceful and has many of the qualities mentioned above. Pausanias refers to statues of Praxiteles in the Attica section of his Guide to Greece (I,20,1-2 — Translated by Peter Levi, S. J. Penguin Books) : *Once when Phryne asked what was his most beautiful work, he promised like a true lover to give it to her, but refused to say which he thought it was. So a servant of Phryne's came rushing in and told him his house was on fire and most of his work was lost. Praxiteles rushed out of doors exclaiming that if the fire had got at the Satyr and the Eros then he had worked for nothing. Phryne told him he could put his mind at rest, nothing horrible had happened except that he was trapped into admitting which was his materpiece. So Phryne chose Eros.* Athenaeus also mentions the statue of Eros (13, 591), saying that Phryne later gave it to her home town, Thespiai. Phryne was the famous Athenian courtesan whom Praxiteles used as the model for the nude Aphrodite of Knidos.

The Hermes was carved out of Parian marble in 343 B.C. and dedicated in the Sacred Altis to commemorate the peace treaty between Eleians and Arcadians. Later it was set up in the Temple of Hera, where it was found during excavations on April 26th, 1877.

The messenger of the gods is shown in the flower of youth carrying the baby Dionysus to the Nymphs of Boeotia. According to

52

legend, Dionysus, god of wine and vineyards, was the son of Zeus and Semele, daughter of Kadmos, King of Thebes. However, when Hera, the faithful consort of Zeus, symbol of conjugal morality and protectress of marriage, heard of Zeus' liaison with Semele, she immediately planned her revenge. Accordingly, she persuaded Semele to ask Zeus to appear before her in all his divine glory after first making him swear an oath. Zeus, bound by the oath, appeared with thunder and lightning which burnt Semele to a cinder, though not before she had given birth prematurely to Dionysus. Zeus then slit open his thigh and put the newborn baby inside it. When the period of pregnancy was over, he gave the baby to Hermes, who, unbeknown to Hera was to entrust it to the care of the Nymphs of Boeotia, or to Ino, Semele's sister, or (in another version) to the Nymphs of the mythical land of Nysa.

During his weary journey, Hermes stopped to rest. Here he leans firmly on his right foot, while the left is relaxed as he turns gracefully to the left. His cloak is draped over the tree trunk on which he is leaning. His right hand, now missing, held a bunch of grapes to attract the attention of little Dionysus, symbolizing the fact that Dionysus was god of wine.

He holds Dionysus and his kerykeion in his left hand which rests on the tree trunk. The Kerykeion (Latin : Caduceus), or herald's staff, is a crozier entwined with serpents symbolizing the messenger and peace. Today, the statue is partly restored in plaster (two legs and the left foot), but the Kerykeion is missing.

The sculptor has portrayed the male body in a very sensitive way by putting most of the weight on the right leg and allowing the left hand to rest on the tree trunk, which he has cleverly covered with the many folds of the cloak. The charming facial expression, the soft cheeks, the beautiful hair and, in general, the tender, youthful skin has been rendered in marble so perfectly that the ideal youth has been created, moving one with his beauty and grace.

It is worth noting how well polished the statue is even today. The back of the statue and the tree trunk were altered in Roman times giving rise to theories that it is a copy, albeit a superb one, of the Praxiteles original. However, most scholars and archaeologists tend to think now that it is an original which was altered in Roman times.

GALLERY IX

Finds of the Roman period (Ist century B.C. to 4th century A.D.) : This is the last period of ancient Greek art when, through Rome, Greek civilisation spread to the West.

Most of the statues in this gallery depict the family of Herodes Atticus, as well as Roman Emperors, their wives, members of their families and various officials, all of which were set up on the Exedra of Herodes Atticus and the Metroön.

The following statues, on the right as we enter the gallery, are worth noting : Roman Emperor Tiberius Claudius (41 - 54 A.D.), as Zeus with an eagle at the base ; Titus (79 - 81 A.D.), in the uniform of a general. The identification of the following statues is not certain : Domitia, wife of Domitian (81 - 96 A.D.), (head missing) ; Agrippina, wife of Tiberius Claudius (41 - 54 A.D.), and the mother of Nero ; Antinoös, the popular favourite of the Emperor Hadrian, who drowned in the Nile because he blindly believed the saying that «by dying a servant prolongs the life of his master». Last is the philhellene, Emperor Hadrian (117 - 138 A.D.), dressed as a general ; during his reign the Sanctuary of Olympia flourished. There are other statues not mentioned here.

The Exedra of Herodes Atticus, where the statues on your left and right were set up, is reconstructed in a drawing. The following whould be noted : Herodes Atticus (101 - 178 A.D.), in a toga (headless) ; Regilla, his wife who was a prietess of Demeter Chamyne (headless) ; the children of Herodes Atticus, etc. Last, in the middle of the gallery, is a marble bull dedicated by the Eleians in honour of Regilla which was set up between the two reservoirs of the aqueduct. It is inscribed as follows : *Regilla, priestess of Demeter (dedicates) the water and everything around it to Zeus.*

The other statues which can be identified are these : The head of the young Emperor Lucius Verus (161 - 169 A.D.) ; Antoninus Pius (138 - 161 A.D.) ; his wife Faustina (torso and head only) ; Faustina the Younger, wife of Marcus Aurelius (161 - 180 A.D.) ; noble Eleian women (Ist century A.D.), all headless ; the head of a noble Eleian woman (Ist century B.C.) ; and last, Poppaea Sabina, Nero's wife (completely preserved).

The cases on the right and left of the gallery display other Roman finds including small bronze objects, the feet of bronze statues, a marble statuette of Aesclepius, terracotta vessels and figurines. Also worthy of note are a complete Corinthian capital and a catalogue of the names of the officials of the Sanctuary from 28 to 24 B.C., inscribed on a marble tile from the roof of the Temple of Zeus.

In the old Museum there still remains a headless statue, two and a half times life-size, of the Roman Emperor Octavian Augustus (30 B.C. to 14 A.D.), which was set up in the Metroön.

GALLERY X

Finds from the Sanctuary connected with the Olympic Games (Geometric to Roman) :
On the left and right of the entrance are two marble statuettes of Nemesis or Divine Retribution (2nd century A.D.), which used to

stand on either side of the exit from the Krypte, the official entrance, to the Stadium.

Next, on the right, are the inscribed marble seat of the Spartan delegate to the Games (second half of the 6th century B.C.), and marble statue bases of Olympic victors of the 4th century B.C.

In one case, there are terracotta and bronze figurines and several other finds of the Geometric period (9th and 8th centuries B.C.), all related to the Olympic games. Next to these, is a fragment of the circular statue base of Kynisca, sister of King Agesilaos II of Sparta (398 - 358 B.C.), which was dedicated in the Altis in 390 - 380 B.C. The inscription refers to her victory in the horse races, where the prizes went not to the charioteers but to the owners themselves.

Amidst a series of statue bases of Olympic champions are two stone dumb-bells (6th century B.C.), which used to be held by the long-jumpers when they performed, and a stone weighing 140 kilos which is inscribed indicating that Vyvon lifted it above his head with one hand.

One of the most interesting bases in the gallery is that of a statue of the famous Olympic champion Poulydamas with relief decoration showing some of his achievments (c. 360 B.C.). Poulydamas, a Thessalian, competed in the Pancration and was world famous for his great strength ; but he died in a cave in an attempt to prevent the roof collapsing.

After the pedestals, there is a case full of bronze statuettes and several small finds, mainly sports equipment like dumb-bells, discuses etc. Amongst these is a statuette of a runner in the starting position (c. 490 B.C.). Note also the Eleian coin (2nd century A.D.), struck on the obverse with a representation of the chryselepantine statue of Zeus by Pheidias, and with the table for the wreaths of the winners on the reverse. Finally, there is a bronze disc of great historical value. It was dedicated to Zeus and is inscribed on both faces. From the one side it is reckoned that the first Olympic Games took place in 776 B.C., while according to the other inscription they took place in 1580 B.C. The higher date of the first Olympics is based on oral tradition.

Next there are two fragments of fossiliferous stone coming from the starting line of the older Classical Stadium.

Finally, after the next case there is the marble grave stele of Kamilos, an Alexandrian athlete, who won a victory at the Nemean Games (3rd century A.D.). It bears an inscription according to which, Kamilos died during a boxing match at the Stadium of Olympia, having asked Zeus to give him the victory wreath or death. This rousing incident shows just how great the honour of an Olympic victory was, since young men did not hesitate to ask the gods for victory or death.

The Pediments and Metopes of the Temple of Zeus are displayed in this gallery. The East Pediment is on the left hand side, the West Pediment on the right side. The Metopes are at either end of the gallery.

AGE AND SCULPTORS OF THE PEDIMENTS

The two pediments belong to the Early Classical period of Greek art (480 - 445 B.C.), and were made during the final years of the construction of the Temple. The building was begun in 470 B.C. and finished in 457 or 456 B.C. This was deduced from a statement in Pausanias (V, 10, 2), where he says that the Spartans dedicated a gold shield in the Temple after the Battle of Tanagra, and recorded the event on a marble plaque attached to the East Pediment, a large part of which has been found.

The Athenians were defeated by the Spartans at the Battle of Tanagra in 457 B.C., and, thus, the gold shield and the inscription must have been dedicated by 455 B.C. at the latest. Work on the Temple and its pediments must have been completed by this date, a conclusion which is reinforced by the style of the pedimental sculptures, themselves, which cannot be later.

Pausanias (V, 10, 8), however, adds confusion by giving another piece of information on the matter, saying that the sculptures of the east pediment were the work of Paionios and those of the west, the work of Alkamenes. Recent historical research, however, has shown this to be incorrect, since not only are the sculptures themselves different in style from the known works of these' two men, but also, they were made when Paionios and Alkamenes were still children.

Thus, the names of the sculptors of the pediments remain a mystery. Were they Athenians, Peloponnesians or, more specifically, Eleians? The fact that the architect of the Temple was Livon of Elis may indicate the latter.

THE EAST PEDIMENT

The East Pediment is on the left of the gallery. There are twenty-one statues in the composition, representing an intriguing myth which took place at Olympia, namely the chariot race between Pelops and Oinomaos.

Oinomaos was supposed to have ruled the ancient city of Pisa, (the modern village of Miraka), which lay one kilometre to the east of the Sanctuary of Olympia. He and his wife, Sterope, had two children, Leukippos and Hippodameia. Leukippos, when he grew up, fell madly in love with the beautiful Daphne, a nymph of Artemis, and daughter of the River Ladon. When she failed to reciprocate his love, Leukippos disguised himself as a nymph to be near his beloved. One day, however, the nymphs decided to bathe together, and, finding Leukippos to be a man, shot him dead with their arrows.

With Leukippos dead, the throne of Pisa had no heir. Meanwhile an oracle had warned Oinomaos that he would be killed before the wedding of his daughter, by the man she was to marry. Thus, Oinomaos proclaimed that any man who wanted the hand of his daughter, Hippodameia, would first have to undergo a trial. This was to take part in a chariot race against Oinomaos, beginning at the Sanctuary of Zeus at Olympia and ending at the Sanctuary of Poseidon on the Isthmus of Corinth. The loser would be killed by the victor. Thus, the prize of the suitor was the beautiful Hippodameia and the sovreignity of Pisa, while for Oinomaos, it was his own life.

However, Oinomaos had issued this challenge because, with his winged horses, he considered himself unbeatable. These horses allowed him to win thirteen races, after each of which he killed the suitor. Then, along came Pelops, rightful son of Tantalus but natural son of Poseidon. The classical myth tells how Pelops asked for the help of Poseidon who gave him four winged horses yolked to a golden chariot, which, according to Pindar, «never tire».

In another version, Hippodameia fell in love with Pelops and for his sake, conspired with her father's charioteer, Myrtilos, against Oinomaos. Knowing that Myrtilos loved her, she offered to reciprocate in return for his cooperation. Thus, Myrtilos removed the linch-pin from Oinomaos' chariot, filling the hole with wax. The wheel soon fell off so fulfilling the oracle.

At any rate, Pelops won, married Hippodameia and celebrated his victory and wedding by holding the Olympic Games in honour of Zeus. Hippodameia, on the other hand, honoured Hera with the consecration of the first Heraia. When Pelops and Hippodameia died, the Pelopion and Hippodameion were set up in their honour, in the Altis.

*

The preparations for the chariot race are shown on the East Pediment. The customary sacrifices have been offered and the contestants are about to start.

The scene is truly moving, since every face reveals the great excitement and anticipation as to the outcome of the race. This anxiety, however, is not a show of dramatic gestures, but remains at a level of «restrained tension» kept under control by lack of movement making the figures appear tragic and in a state of deep concentration.

The East Pediment

Let us now look at each statue in turn following the letters and numbers on the diagram.

M : The majestic figure in the centre is Zeus. The god is standing between the two opponents, the invisible judge of the race which is about to start. His left hand holds his thunderbolt while his right simply touches his cloak. The head is missing.

1 : On Zeus' right is Oinomaos the legendary king of Pisa. A spear is held in his left hand while his right rests on his hip, with two fingers arrogantly bent back. Victory is assured. His proud mein and haughty stance show that he has complete faith in his own strength and that of his horses.

2 : Next to Oinomaos stands Sterope, his faithful wife and woeful mother of Hippodameia. Her Doric peplos lends her the dignity of a noblewoman.

3 : A groom is tending Oinomaos' horses next to Sterope, and kneels before them.

4 : Behind the groom are the four horses of Oinomaos ; their chariot, said to have been of bronze, is missing. It may have been painted onto the now destroyed tympanum.

5 : A kneeling figure behind the horses may be Myrtilos, Oinomaos' charioteer.

6 : Next is another male figure, perhaps an soothsayer.

7 : Lastly, a muscular young man lying down, is the personification of the River Alpheios.

a : To the left of Zeus stands Pelops, spear in his right hand, and shield in his left. His bronze breastplate was attached to the small holes in the chest. He is an imposing figure with the youthful, lithe body of an athlete, but uncertainty as to the outcome of the race is reflected in his expression and the tilt of his head.

b : Hippodameia stands next to Pelops, raising her left hand in embarrassment as if to arrange the folds of her Doric peplos.

c : A maid-servant kneels before Hippodameia, her head bowed.

d : Behind the maid are the four horses of Pelops. Again the chariot is missing ; like the other, this would either have been made of bronze or painted on the tympanum of the Temple.

e : Next to the horses is the magnificent figure of an old man. This is «the old thinker», that is to say the soothsayer whose pained expression heightens the tragedy of the moment. In his left hand he held a stick (which does not survive), while his right is stroking his

58

thick beard, as he forsees the great tragedy about to befall the House of Oinomaos.

f : Next to the old man, is the figure of an exquisite boy who is gazing at his left foot apparently unaware of his surroundings.

g : The last figure is the personification of the Kladeos River as an attractive young man. The fact that two rivers, the Kladeos and the Alpheios are placed at either side of the pediment, symbolizes that the chariot-race took place in Olympia through which they flow.

THE WEST PEDIMENT

The West Pediment is on the right of the gallery. This pediment also comprises twenty-one figures all intertwined into a lovely composition, representing a panhellenic myth, namely the battle between the Laptiths and Centaurs.

According to the myth, Ixion had committed a crime and begged Zeus for mercy. Zeus forgave him and invited him to dinner. However, the ungrateful man tried to flirt with Hera. Zeus was unable to bear the insult, and, taking a cloud, transformed it into the shape of Hera. Ixion approached her, and from their intercourse, the father of the Centaurs was born.

The Centaurs, which were half man, half horse, lived on Mount Pelion in Thessaly close to the brave warrion Lapiths. Once, King Peirithous of the Lapiths wanted to celebrate his wedding to Deidameia who is called Hippodameia by some scholars though she has no connection with the heroine of the East Pediment. Peirithous then invited his friend Theseus and his neighbours, the Centaurs to honour the wedding with their presence. During the feast which followed, the Centaurs became drunk and their king Eurytion offended the bride Deidameia. The Lapiths were furious and dragged Eurytion out and cut off his nose and ears.

Homer, in the Odyssey, describes the scene as follows :

> *...It was the wine that got at his wits in King Peirithous'*
> *house, when he was visiting the Lapithae. Fuddled with*
> *drink what must he do but run amuck in the palace? His*
> *host leapt up in anger, dragged him to the porch, and*
> *threw him out of doors; but not before they had sliced*
> *his ears and nose off with a knife.*

(*Odyssey, Book XXI, 294-301* — Translated by E.V. Rieu, Methuen).

Meantime, the other Centaurs, armed with rocks and huge trees, attacked the Lapiths and tried to steal away their wives and children. The Lapiths, with the help of Theseus, bravely confronted their attackers with swords. At length, the Centaurs were defeated and put to flight in total disorder pursued by the Lapiths to the foot of Mount Pindus. Thus, honour and justice were satisfied.

*

The climax of this mythical battle, with successive scenes of violence and brutality, is depicted on the West Peiment. The whole composition provides an accurate picture of devastating tragedy. Several of the groups are worth examining in detail :

M : Apollo «of the golden locks», which was the epithet given him by the Ancient Greeks, was worshipped particularly in Thessaly, where this battle is supposed to have taken place, which explains his presence here. He stands in the centre invisible to the two opposing sides. His Olympian tranquillity, beauty and strength denote the presence of a god. In his left hand he held a bow and arrow (missing), while his right hand is calmly outstretched personifying divine goodness and it is as if he wants to put an end to the evil of war, to punish injustice and restore order.

1 : To the right of Apollo is one of the most beautiful groups in this composition : Centaur Eurytion carrying off the bride Deidameia. His right fore-limb embraces the beautiful body of the queen. With his left hand he grabs her breast, while his right holds fast her waist. The small holes which one can distinguish on his head were probably used to attach a golden crown, presumably to distinguish the king of the Centaurs from the rest. Therefore one concludes that the woman he is abducting must be Deidameia, since accordint to the myth, it was Deidameia that Eurytion assaulted.

Deidameia is struggling to protect herself. Her right hand is pushing the Centaur's hand away. Her left hand is trying to cover her breast, while she thrusts back the Centaur's head with her elbow. Deidameia's exquisite beauty and the sweetness of her face contrast with the wild expression of the Centaur, and her expression manifests a sense of shame for her predicament.

Little remains of the figure of Peirithous (only the head and a few fragments of the limbs), but he is shown standing beside the Centaur's back legs, ready to kill the aggressor with his sword.

2 : Next to this group is another, badly damaged, which depicts a Centaur abducting a young Lapith boy.

3 : In the midst of the next group, a Centaur is seizing a Lapith woman by her hair. She courageously repulses him and at the same time a Lapith knocks the Centaur to his knees.

4 : Further on, a terrified Lapith woman has fallen to the ground, but her eyes are still fixed on the battle.

5 : At the corner is another fallen figure of a Lapith woman, watching the battle in terror.

This completes the description of the left hand half of the pediment.

The West Pediment

a : To the left of Apollo is another interesting group. A Lapith woman (head missing), fights off a Centaur. She is so desperate that her nails dig deep into his cheek. The Centaur recoils in pain, screaming and, with his right fore-limb raised in fury, he kicks her on the knee.

Theseus, Peirithous loyal friend, is standing behind the Centaur, an axe raised in both hands ready to strike the Centaur.

b : Next to this group, another Centaur and a Lapith are in mortal combat. The Lapith has the Centaur's neck in the crook of his arm trying to strangle him. The Centaur is biting into the Lapith's flesh. But the Lapith endeavours to hold his ground ; forehead furrowed by two deep wrinkles, biting his tongue, his expression is one of extreme pain.

c : Another group, in the centre, represents the seizing of a Lapith woman by a Centaur. She bravely thrusts him backwards. A little further away, a Lapith has stabbed a Centaur with a dagger which has completely penetrated his chest and come out through his right shoulder blade. The holes which can be seen at that point were for attaching the bronze dagger.

d : Next to this group is a Lapith woman who has fallen down and is staring at the battle in horror.

e : Lastly, at the corner, there is another fallen figure of a Lapith woman, which completes the magnificent composition of the Pediment.

THE METOPES OF THE TEMPLE OF ZEUS

The twelve metopes of the Temple of Zeus, which depict the twelve labours of Hercules, are on exhibition in the Central Gallery.

Hercules, son of Zeus and Alkmene, was a panhellenic hero, whose bravery, craftiness and strength made him a symbol for young athletes and sportsmen, which is why myths related to his labours greatly appealed to the Greeks.

As mentioned above in the description of the Temple, the metopes were placed in groups of six on the frieze over the entrances to the prodomos and the opisthodomos. The metopes in the gallery are exhibited in specially constructed triglyphs, in the same order that they were placed in the temple.

On entering the gallery, exhibited opposite from left to right are the 6 metopes of the opisthodomos, depicting the first six labours of Hercules.

In the first metope, Hercules who has already killed the Lion of Nemea in his first labour, is shown as a very young hero. Exhausted after the struggle, he has placed his foot on the dead lion (only a small fragment of the lower part of the animal survives), and rests his head on his right hand. The goddess Athena (only the head is preserved), his patroness, stands before him. The rest of the sculpture is a gypsum reproduction of the original, now in the Louvre, where it was taken together with other finds, after the French excavations in 1829.

Only a few pieces of the next metope, depicting the slaying of the Lernaian Hydra, the second Labour of Hercules, survive.

In the third metope, Hercules offers the Birds of Stymphalus to the goddess Athena. She with the sweet expression of a young girl, is sitting on a rock and moves her right hand to accept the offer of her protégé. Except for Hercules' torso, the metope is a gypsum copy of the original in the Louvre.

In the fourth metope, Hercules who appears with a club in his right hand, has vanquished the Cretan Bull. Apart from the bull's head and fragments of Hercules' hands, the greater part of the original is in the Louvre.

Very few fragments of the fifth and sixth metopes survive. In the fifth labour, Hercules captures the Hind of Ceryneia. In the sixth labour, he kills Hyppolyta, the Amazon, and seizes her girdle.

The six metopes of the prodomos, opposite the previous series, are exhibited in order from left to right.

Only a few fragments of the first, second and third metopes survive. In the first, Hercules carries on his shoulders the Boar of Erymanthus frightening Eurysteus. In the second he beats the Horses of Diomedes with his club. In the third he battles with and kills the triple-bodied monster Geryon.

The fourth metope is in very good condition. It shows Hercules in the centre, supporting the Heavens on his shoulders, until Atlas arrives to offer him the Golden Apples of the Hesperides. Athena stands behind Hercules, assisting him with her left hand.

In the fifth metope Hercules is dragging Cerberus, the appalling triple-headed dog who guarded the gates of Hell. At the right side of the metope, stood Hermes, who had accompanied Hercules on his descent to the underworld and his return to the light of day.

The last metope portrays an important local myth, mentioned in the Introduction. This is the myth of Hercules cleaning the Stables of Augeias. The goddess Athena stands next to Hercules, fully armed with spear and shield, helping him. One version of the myth says that Hercules joined the rivers of Elis, the Alpheios and Peneios, to flow in one channel and pass through the stables, so making his task easier.

PLATES

Αναπαράσταση του Ιερού της Ολυμπίας
Model of the Sanctuary of Olympia
Maquette du Sanctuaire d' Olympie
Modell des Heiligtums von Olympia
Plastico del Santuario di Olimpia
Maqueta del Santuario de Olimpia

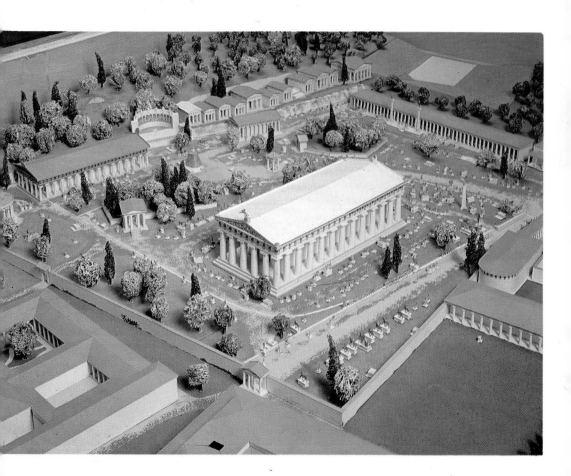

Παλαίστρα
e Palaestra
Palestre
e Palästra
Palestra
Palestra
▷

▷
Φιλιππείο
e Philippeion
Philippeion
s Philippeion
Philippeion
Filipeio.

◁

ναός της Ήρας
e Temple of Hera
Temple d' Héra
r Heratempel
tempio di Era
Templo de Hera

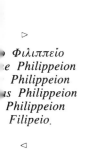

·Ο δρόμος προς τις αρχαιότητ
ο Κρόνιος Λόφος
The road to the Site and
Kronos Hill
Le chemin conduisant au site
et le Mont Kronion
Der Weg zu den Ruinen un
Kronos - Hügel
Il colle Cronion e la via ch
duce alla zona archeolo
El camino hacia las antigüeda
el monte Crono

◁

Το Γυμνάσιο
The Gymnasium
Le Gymnase
Das Gymnasion
Il Ginnasio
El Gimnasio

▷

Εξέδρα Ηρώδη του Αττι
Exedra of Herodes Attic
Exèdre d' Hérode Atticus
Exedra des Herodes Atti
Esedra di Erode Attico
Exedra de Herodes Atico

Αθήνα - Εθνικό Μουσείο: Χάλκινη κεφαλή πυγμάχου, που βρέθηκε
στην Ολυμπία (340 π.Χ. περίπου)
Athens - National Museum: Bronze head of a boxer found at Olympia
(c. 340 B.C.)
Athènes - Musée National: Tête en bronze d' un pugiliste, trouvée à
Olympie (340 av. J.-C. env.)
Athen, Nationalmuseum: Kopf eines Faustkämpfers, Bronze, gefunden
in Olympia (ca. 340 v.Chr.)
Atene - Museo Nazionale: Testa di bronzo di pugile, trovata ad
Olimpia (c. 340 a.C.)
Atenas - Museo Nacional: Cabeza de bronce del pugilista, encontrada
en Olimpia (340 a.C. aprox.)

Κεφαλή Ήρας (600 - 560 π.Χ.)
Head of Hera (600 - 560 B.C.)
Tête d' Héra (600 - 560 av. J.-C.)
Kopf der Hera (600 - 560 v.Chr.)
Testa di Era (600 - 560 a.C.)
Gabeza de Hera (600 - 560 a.C.)

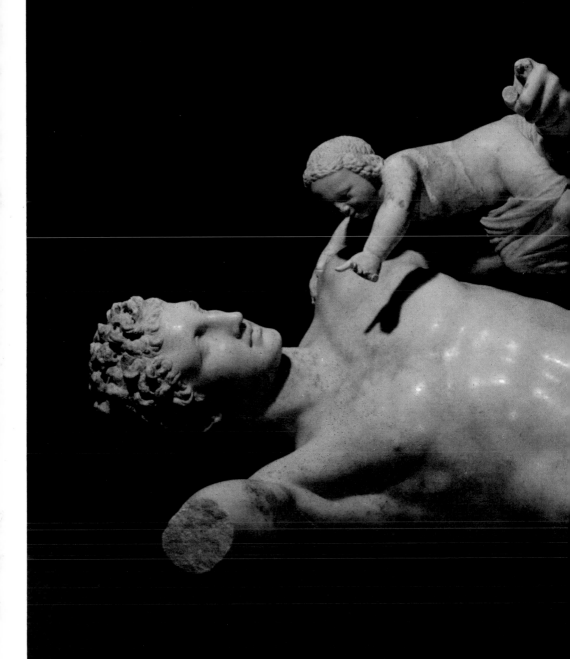

O Ερμῆς του Πραξιτέλη   Hermes of Praxiteles   Hermès de Praxitèle   Hermes des Praxiteles   Ermes di Prassitele   Hermes de Praxiteles

Η Κρυπτή
The Krypte
Le passage voûté
Die Krypta
La Cripta
La Cripta

Εξέδρα Ηρώδη του Αττικού
Exedra of Herodes Atticus
Exèdre d' Hérode Atticus
Exedra des Herodes Attikus
Esedra di Erode Attico
Exedra de Herodes Atico

Ο ναός του Δία
The Temple of Zeus
Le Temple de Zeus
Der Zeustempel
Il tempio di Zeus
El Templo de Zeus

Ο ναός του Δία
The Temple of Zeus
Le Temple de Zeus
Der Zeustempel
Il tempio di Zeus
El Templo de Zeus

Ο Ερμής του Πραξιτέλη
Hermes of Praxiteles
Hermès de Praxitèle

Hermes des Praxiteles
Ermes di Prassitele
Hermes de Praxiteles

Ο Απόλλωνας (Δ. Αέτωμα)   Apollon (Westgiebel)
Apollo (W. Pediment)   Apollo (Frontone occ.)
Apollon (Fronton O.)   Apolo (Frontón occ.)

Γενική άποψη του Ιερού
General view of the Sanctuary
Vue générale du Sanctuaire
Ansicht des Heiligtums von Olympia
Vista generale di Santuario
Vista general del Santuario

Γενική ἀποψη τῆς Κρυπτῆς
General view of the Krypte
Vue générale du passage voûté
Blick auf die Krypta
Vista generale della Cripta
Vista general de la Cripta

ναός της Ἥρας
Temple of Hera
Temple d' Héra
Heratempel
Tempio di Era
Templo de Hera

◁ ▷

▷

Βουλευτήριο
Bouleuterion
Bouleutérion
Bouleuterion
Bouleuterion
Buleuterio

Ο Δίας απάγει το Γανυμηδη   Zeus entführt Ganymed
The Rape of Ganymedes by Zeus   Zeus che rapisce Ganimede
Zeus et Ganymède   Zeus raptando a Ganimedes

◁

Η Παλαίστρα
The Palaestra
La Palestre
Die Palästra
La Palestra
La Palestra

△ Η Κρυπτή
The Krypte
Le passage voûté
Die Krypta
La Cripta
▽ La Cripta

Γενική ἄποψη τῆς κοιλάδας τῆς Ολυμπίας   *General view of the valley of Olympia*   *Vue générale de la*

Das Tal von Olympia   Vista generale della valle di Olimpia   Vista general del valle de Olimpia

Η Κρυπτή   Die Krypta
The Krypte   La Cripta
Le passage voûté   La Cripta

Το Στάδιο   Das Stadion
The Stadium   Lo Stadio
Le Stade   El Estadio

▷

◁

Κεφαλή γρύπα από χαλκό (7ος αι. π.Χ.)
Head of griffin (Bronze, 7th C. B.C.)
Tête de griffon (Bronze, 7e s. av. J.-C.)
Greifenkopf (Bronze, 7. Jh. v.Chr.)
Testa di grifone (Bronzo, VII s. a.C.)
Cabeza de grifo (Bronce, s. VII a.C.)

Περσικό Κράνος (500 - 480 π.Χ.)
Persian Helmet (500 - 480 B.C.)
Casque perse (500 - 480 av. J.-C.)
Persischer Helm (500 - 480 v.Chr.)
Elmo persiano (500 - 480 a.C.)
Yelmo Persa (500 - 480 a.C.)

Γρύπας από χαλκό (7ος αι. π.Χ.)   Greif (Bronze, 7. Jh. v. Chr.)
Griffin (Bronze, 7th C. B.C.)   Grifone (Bronzo, VII s. a.C.)
Griffon (Bronze, 7e s. av. J.-C.)   Grifo (Bronce, s. VII a.C.)

Κράνος (620 - 580 π.Χ.)
Helmet (620 - 580 B.C.)
Casque (620 - 580 av. J.-C.)
Helm (620 - 580 v.Chr.)
Elmo (620 - 580 a.C.)
Yelmo (620 - 580 a.C.)

Κεφαλή γρύπα από χαλκό (6ος αι. π.Χ.)
Head of griffin (Bronze, 6th C. B.C.)
Tête de griffon (Bronze, 6e s. av. J.-C.)
Greifenkopf (Bronze, 6. Jh. v.Chr.)
Testa di grifone (Bronzo, VI s. a.C.)
Cabeza de grifo (Bronce, s. VI a.C.)

Το Κράνος του Μιλτιάδη   Helm des Miltiades
The Helmet of Miltiades   Elmo di Milziade
Le casque de Miltiade   El casco de Miltiades

Κεφαλή γυναίκας (520 - 500 π.Χ.)
Head of woman (520 - 500 B.C.)
Tête de Femme (520 - 500 av. J.-C.)
Frauenkopf (520 - 500 v.Chr.)
Testa femminile (520 - 500 a.C.)
Cabeza de mujer (520 - 500 a.C.)

Αθηνά (Πήλινο, 490 π.Χ. περίπου)
Athena (Terracotta, c. 490 B.C.)
Athéna (Terre cuite, 490 av. J.-C. env.)
Athena (Terrakotta, ca. 490 v.Chr.)
Atena (Terracotta c. 490 a.C.)
Atenea (Terracota, 490 a.C. aprox.)

Η Νίκη του Παιωνίου
The Nike of Paionios
La Victoire de Paeonio
Die Nike des Paionios
La Nike di Peonio
La Victoria de Paionio
◁

▷
Αναπαράσταση της Νίκ
The Reconstruction of Ν
Reconstitution de la Vic
Rekonstruktion der Nike
Ricostruzione della Nike
Reproducción de la Vic

◁

Ο Ερμής του Πραξιτέλη	Hermes des Praxiteles	Αντίνοος Antinoos
Hermes of Praxiteles	Ermes di Prassitele	Antinoös Antinoo
Hermès de Praxitèle	Hermes de Praxiteles	Antinoüs Antinoo

△

Μετόπη : Οι Στυμφαλίδες Όρνιθες
Metope : The Stymphalian Birds
Métope : Les Oiseaux du Stymphale
Metope : Die stymphalischen Vögel
Metopa : Gli uccelli di Stimfalia
Metopa : Los Pájaros de Estinfalia

Μετόπη : Αναγωγή
          του Κέρβερου
Metope : Cerberus
Métope : Cerbère
Metope : Kerberos
Metopa : Cerbero
Metopa : Cerbero

Η Παλαίστρα   The Palaestra   La Pales

Die Palästra   La Palestra   La Palestra

Ο Δίας του Φειδία σε νόμισμα των Ηλείων
Pheidias's Zeus, representation on a coin of Eleians
Le Zeus de Phidias sur une pièce de monnaie d' Elis
Zeus des Pheidias auf Münzen von Elis
Lo Zeus di Fidia su una moneta di Elide
Zeus de Fidias según una moneda de Elis

Υδρορρόη του ναού του Δία   Wasserspeier vom Zeustempel
Gargoyle from the Temple of Zeus   Grondaia del tempio di Zeus
Gargouille du temple de Zeus   Cárgola del templo de Zeus

Μικρή οινοχόη του Φειδία
The cup of Pheidias
La coupe de Phidias
Kännchen des Pheidias
La tazza di Fidia
La copa de Fidias

Υδρορρόη του ναού του Δία   Wasserspeier vom Zeustempel
Gargoyle from the Temple of Zeus   Grondaia del tempio di Zeus
Gargouille du temple de Zeus   Cárgola del templo de Zeus

Αλογάκι από χαλκό
  (460 π.Χ. περίπου)
Statuette of a Horse
  (Bronze, c. 460 B.C.)
Statuette de cheval
  (Bronze, 460 av. J.-C. env.)
Pferdestatuette
  (Bronze, ca. 460 v. Chr.)
Cavallo
  (Bronzo, c. 460 a.C.)
Caballo
  (Bronce, 460 a.C. aprox.)
      ◁ ▷

      ▷
Αλογάκι από χαλκό
  (7ος αι. π.Χ.)
Statuette of a Horse
  (Bronze, 7th C. B.C.)
Statuette de cheval
  (Bronze, 7e s. av. J.-C.)
Pferdestatuette
  (Bronze, 7. Jh. v. Chr.)
Cavallo
  (Bronzo, VII s. a.C.)
Caballo
  (Bronce, s. VII a.C.)

Η Δηιδάμεια (Δ. Αέτωμα)   Deidameia (Westgiebel)
Deidameia (W. Pediment)   Deidamia (Frontone occ.)
Déidamie (Fronton O.)   Deidamia (Frontón occ.)

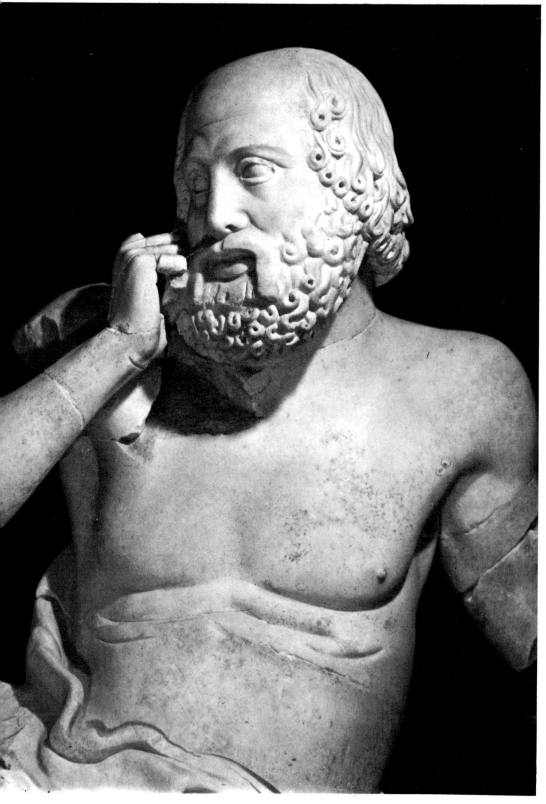

Ο Σύννους Γέρων (Α. Αέτωμα)   *Der greise Seher (Ostgiebel)*
The Old Thinker (E. Pediment)   *Il vecchio pensieroso (Frontone or.)*
Le vieillard pensif (Fronton E.)   *El viejo pensador (Frontón or.)*

Ο Οινόμαος (Α. Αἐτωμα)
Oinomaos (E. Pediment)
Oenomaos (Fronton E.)
Oinomaos (Ostgiebel)
Enomao (Frontone or.)
Enomao (Frontón or.)

Ο Πέλοπας (Α. Αέτωμα)
Pelops (E. Pediment)
Pélops (Fronton E.)
Pelops (Ostgiebel)
Pelope (Frontone or.)
Pélope (Frontón or.)

Ανατολικὸ Αέτωμα: Μορφὲς 4 καὶ 3
East Pediment: Figures 4 and 3
Fronton Est: Figures 4 et 3

Ostgiebel: Figuren 4 und 3
Frontone orientale: Figure 4 e 3
Frontón oriental : Figuras 4 y 3

Ανατολικό Αέτωμα: Μορφές γ και δ
East Pediment: Figures c and d
Fronton Est: Figures c et d

Ostgiebel: Figuren c und d
Frontone orientale : Figure c e d
Frontón oriental : Figuras c y d

Η Στερόπη (Α. Αέτωμα)
Sterope (E. Pediment)
Stéropé (Fronton E.)
Sterope (Ostgiebel)
Sterope (Frontone or.)
Estérope (Frontón or.)

Η Ιπποδάμεια (Α. Αέτωμα)
Hippodameia (E. Pediment)
Hippodamie (Fronton E.)
Hippodameia (Ostgiebel)
Ippodamia (Frontone or.)
Hipodamia (Frontón or.)

Λαπιθίδα (Μορφή 4, Δ. Αέτωμα)
Lapith woman (Figure 4, W. Pediment)
Femme Lapithe (Figure 4, Fronton occ.)

Lapithin (Figur 4, Westgiebel)
Donna lapita (Figura 4, Frontone occ.)
Mujer Lapita (Figura 4, Frontón occ.)

Ο Αλφειός (Μορφή 7, Α. Αέτωμα)
Alpheios (Figure 7, E. Pediment)
Alphée (Figure 7, Fronton E.)

Alpheios (Figur 7, Ostgiebel)
Alfeo (Figura 7, Frontone or.)
Alfeo (Figura 7, Frontón or.)

Lapithin (Figur d, Westgiebel)
Donna lapita (Figura d, Frontone occ.)
Mujer Lapita (Figura d, Frontón occ.)

Λαπιθίδα (Μορφή δ´, Δ. Ἀέτωμα)
Lapith woman (Figure d, W. Pediment)
Femme Lapithe (Figure d, Fronton O.)

Ὁ Κλάδεος (Μορφή ζ, Α. Ἀέτωμα)
Kladeos (Figure g, E. Pediment)
Kladéos (Figure g, Fronton E.)

Kladeos (Figur g, Ostgiebel)
Cladeo (Figura g, Frontone or.)
Cladeo (Figura g, Frontón or.)

Σύμπλεγμα 1 (Δ. Ἀέτωμα)   Gruppe 1 (Westgiebel)
Group 1 (W. Pediment)   Gruppo 1 (Frontone occ.)
Groupe 1 (Fronton O.)   Grupo 1 (Frontón occ.)

Σύμπλεγμα α (Δ. Αέτωμα)   Gruppe a (Westgiebel)
Group a (W. Pediment)   Gruppo a (Frontone occ.)
Groupe a (Fronton O.)   Grupo a (Frontón occ.)

πιθίδα (Σύμπλεγμα 3, Δ. Αέτωμα)
•ith woman (Group 3, W. Pediment)
•me Lapithe (Groupe 3, Fronton O.)
•ithin (Gruppe 3, Westgiebel)
•na lapita (Gruppo 3, Frontone occ.)
•ier Lapita (Grupo 3, Frontón occ.)

Δ
Κεφαλὴ Κενταύρου (Σύμπλεγμα 3, Δ. Αέτωμα)
Head of Centaur (Group 3, W. Pediment)
Tête de Centaure (Groupe 3, Fronton O.)
Kentaurenkopf (Gruppe 3, Westgiebel)
Testa di Centauro (Gruppo 3, Frontone occ.)
Cabeza de Centauro (Grupo 3, Frontón occ.)

Λαπιθίδα (Σύμπλεγμα γ , Δ. Αέτωμα)   Lapithin (Gruppe c, Westgiebel)
Lapith woman (Group c, W. Pediment)   Donna lapita (Gruppo c, Frontone occ.)
Femme Lapithe (Groupe c, Fronton O.)   Mujer Lapita (Grupo c, Frontón occ.)

Σύμπλεγμα б (Δ. Αέτωμα)   Gruppe b (Westigiebel)
Group b (W. Pediment)   Gruppo b (Frontone occ.)
Groupe b (Fronton O.)   Grupo b (Frontón occ.)

ιππίνα (;) μητέρα του Νέρωνα
ppina (?) mother of Nero
ppine (?) mère de Néron
ppina (?) Mutter des Nero
ppina (?) madre di Nerone
pina (?) madre de Nerón
▷

◁
υτοκράτορας Αδριανός
eror Hadrian
ien, Empereur Romain
ian, römischer Kaiser
nperatore Adriano
ano, Emperador de Roma